The Seven I Am Of Jesus

The Seven I Am Of Jesus

Kerney Thomas

The Seven I Am Of Jesus
ISBN: 979-8-9883949-1-4
All Rights Reserved.

Copyright © 2025 by Dirk A. Thomas

No part of this book may be reproduced or transmitted in any form or by any means, graphic, electronic, or mechanical, including photocopying, recording, taping or by any information storage or retrieval system, without the permission in writing from the author or publisher.

Unless otherwise indicated, all scripture quotations are from the King James Version of the Bible.

Published and edited by:
Ronnie J. Wells Publishing
P.O. Box 90151
Atlanta, Georgia 30364
(678) 416-8325
adonai314@yahoo.com

Cover Art by: Phanazz Concepts
(404) 579-8019

Logo Art by: Paul Clark
paulclark.pc44@gmail.com

Printed in the United States of America.
All Rights Reserved under International Copyright Law.

TABLE OF CONTENTS

ଔଓ

Dedication 1
Synopsis 2
Introduction 3
Acknowledgments 6
Special Acknowledgments 7
A Journey of Transformation 9

Chapter 1
Unveiling the Seven 'I Am' Statements of Jesus: Discovering Yourself in the Identity of Jesus . . 10

JESUS WHO AM: Am I asking Jesus who I am or is Jesus telling me who He is? 11

Revealed: The Profound Meaning Behind Jesus' Seven 'I Am' Declarations 11

1. Jesus said, "I am the bread of life: Nourishment for the Soul." 12

2. Jesus said, "I am the light of the world: Illuminating Truth and Grace." 18

3. Jesus said, "I am the gate for the sheep: Welcoming All to the Flock." 25

4. Jesus said, "I am the Good Shepherd: Guiding and Protecting His Flock." 31

5. Jesus said, "I am the resurrection and the life: Hope Beyond Death." 37

6. Jesus said I am the way the truth and the life: Pathway to Redemption." 43

7. Jesus said. "I am the true Vine: Bearing Fruit in
   Abundance." 49

Chapter 2
Embracing Jesus Seven "I Am" Statement: Jesus the Seven I am **56**

The clarity of Jesus 59

Jesus Seven I am finding myself in the context of Jesus . 59

Jesus, the Seven I am exclusive to Jesus ONLY . . 61

Confession unto Jesus 62

Chapter 3
I Can See Clearly Now: The Oneness of Jesus and Man **65**

Divine Encounter: Surrendering to The I Am . . 68

Jesus said we are joint heirs with Him . . . 71

Joint heirs: not of the world 73

Joint heirs: Reflection of The Light . . . 75

Joint heirs: Reflection of The Door . . . 82

Joint heirs: Reflection of The Good Shepherd . 86

Joint heirs: Reflection of The Resurrection and the Life . 91

Joint heirs: Reflection of The Way, The Truth,
and The Life 96

Joint heirs: Reflection of The True Vine . . . 101

Joint heirs: Reflection of The 7 I Am . . . 105

Joint heirs: The 7 I am Statements and
1 Corinthians 3:6-9 108

Living as the Bread of Life	114
Living as the Light of the World	116
Living as the Door	117
Living as the Good Shepherd	120
Living as the Resurrection and the Life	122
Living as the Way, the Truth, and the Life	124
Living as the Vine	126
We are Ambassador for Christ	128
The appointment as an "Ambassador for Christ"	131

Chapter 4
A Journey of Transformation through Romans 10:9 . **135**

Awakening to Redemption: The Power of Confession	137
The Transformation of Confession.	139
Rediscovering a Life testimony: Dirk Thomas From Darkness to Light	142
Seeing Jesus in the testimony Connecting to the "I am" statements of Jesus	144
Welcome into the Family of Faith	146
TESTIMONY: The Kerney Thomas story told by Dirk Thomas	147
I'm blessed, good-looking, have plenty of money, and I am the love of God.	151
Matthew 17:20 broken down to a step-by-step process in a person's life	159

TESTIMONY: I am what I am by choice or mistake. . 161
Your Purpose and Benefit 167

Chapter 5
The Threefold Journey: Surrender, Transformation, and Responsibility in Light of the Seven Identities of Jesus — 171

Three stage process surrender transformation responsibility:
The Concept of Surrendering to the Identity of Jesus . 174

Transformation through Surrender to Christ: Unveiling the
Essence of Being 176

Fulfilling the Covenant: Embracing Responsibility in Unity
with the Creator 179

Take a marvelous journey with Jesus. . . . 181

As I walk 185

A lifetime Journey 187

Stage 1: Surrendering to Jesus Christ . . . 188

Stage 2: Experiencing Transformation . . . 188

Stage 3: Bearing Fruit and Sharing the Experience . . 188

Alignment with the Word of God . . . 189

Chapter 6
THE FOUR PHASES OF WHO AM I . . 191

Phase 1. Personal Authenticity: Embracing Your True Self . 194

Phase 2. External Perceptions: The Mirror of Society . 199

How to balance seeking validation from others and staying
true to yourself 202

How to establish boundaries with people who are constantly

seeking your validation	206
The importance of self-validation versus external validation: The foundation of self-worth and personal growth. .	211
Phase 3. Divine Perspective: A Higher Gaze . .	216
When God calls my name	224
Phase 4. Profound nature of Jesus' identity and mission .	224
Final words	234
About The Author	235
Contact The Author	237

Dedication

ෆ⊗

This book is dedicated in loving memory of Pastor Michael Robinson Sr. (December 23, 1961 - August 20, 2024) and his devoted wife, Elder Marlesa Robinson (March 18, 1956 - November 10, 2024) of Little Miller Grove Baptist Church, 1970 Peters Road, Tucker, Georgia. Your unwavering support and encouragement continue to inspire this journey.

Synopsis

☙❧

"The Seven I Am of Jesus" is a transformative exploration into the profound relationship between understanding Jesus and discovering your own identity. This insightful book delves into the seven significant declarations made by Jesus, each revealing His divine nature and purpose. Therefore, discovering your divine nature and purpose.

As readers journey through these revelations, they are invited to reflect on their personal relationship with Christ. In understanding who Jesus is, individuals gain clearer insight into their own character and authenticity. Rooted in scripture, this book offers a path to self-discovery through a spiritual lens, encouraging readers to embrace their true selves.

As a result, readers will walk away with a deepened sense of fulfillment and an enhanced perspective on their personal life, grounded in the enlightening truth of God's word.

Introduction

In the Bible, Matthew 16:15, Jesus asks His disciples, "But what about you?" he asked. "Who do you say I am?" This question is significant because it highlights the importance of personal revelation and understanding of one's identity and beliefs.

The disciples' responses to Jesus' question reflect the diversity of opinions concerning His identity. "Some say that you are John the Baptist, others Elijah, and still others Jeremiah or one of the prophets." This diversity highlights the varying perceptions and understandings people have about Jesus. Some saw Him as a teacher, others as a revolutionary leader, and some even compared Him to the great prophets of the past. This diversity of opinions speaks to the complex and multifaceted nature of Jesus and the perceptions people hold about Him.

The significance of this question lies in the implications it has for personal faith and understanding. Just as the disciples were asked to articulate their beliefs about Jesus, each individual is called to consider their own understanding of who Jesus is. This introspective process can help individuals deepen their faith and develop a more personal and meaningful relationship with Jesus.

The importance of people seeing Jesus and understanding who they think He is, is crucial for their spiritual journey and growth. Without a clear understanding of who Jesus is to them personally, individuals may struggle to fully connect with Him and His message. Developing a personal understanding with Jesus allows for a more profound and transformative experience of faith, one that goes beyond mere adherence to a set of beliefs and becomes a deeply rooted aspect of one's identity.

Understanding who Jesus is also plays a crucial role in shaping one's values, beliefs, and actions. If an individual sees Jesus as a teacher of love, compassion, and forgiveness, they are more likely to embody these traits in their own lives. On the other hand, if someone sees Jesus as a revolutionary figure challenging the status quo, they may be inspired to advocate for justice and social change. Therefore, the perception of who Jesus is directly influences how individuals navigate their own lives and interact with the world around them.

Furthermore, the question of who Jesus is serves as a foundation for individuals to understand themselves. Just as the disciples were asked about their perception of Jesus, each person is called to reflect on their own identity and beliefs. This introspective process allows individuals to explore their values, motivations, and understanding of the divine. In turn, this self-reflection can lead to a deeper sense of purpose, identity, and meaning in life.

Knowing who you are, in the context of understanding Jesus, is essential for personal growth and spiritual development. By engaging with the question of who Jesus is, individuals are prompted to consider how their beliefs and perceptions shape their understanding of themselves. This self-awareness can lead to a more authentic and integrated sense of identity, as individuals align their beliefs with their actions and values.

As individuals develop a deeper understanding of who they believe Jesus to be, they can also uncover aspects of their own character and belief system. This process of self-discovery is essential for personal growth and contributes to a more fulfilling and purposeful life. Understanding who Jesus is serves as a springboard for individuals to explore their own beliefs, values, and aspirations, leading to a more profound sense of self-understanding and personal identity.

In conclusion, the question of who Jesus is goes beyond mere theological debate; it is a deeply personal and transformative inquiry that has the power to shape an individual's faith, values, and sense of self. By engaging with this question, individuals are encouraged to develop a personal relationship with Jesus, one that goes beyond surface-level perceptions and delves into the core of their beliefs and identity. This process of self-discovery and faith formation is essential for personal growth and spiritual development. Therefore, the question of who Jesus is holds profound significance for individuals as they seek to understand themselves and their place in the world.

Acknowledgments

I am deeply grateful for the incredible support and generosity shown by everyone, including businesses, which believed in my financial venture of writing this book. To each of you who have contributed to making "The 7 I Am of Jesus" a reality, your support has been an unwavering source of encouragement and faith in my vision. Your kindness and belief in my work have not only brought this project to life but have also enriched my journey tremendously.

I am truly inspired by your generosity and commitment to helping bring this message to others. May your kindness be abundantly rewarded, and may this book inspire and bless all who read it as much as your support has blessed me. Thank you from the bottom of my heart!

Special Acknowledgments

William P. Evans
Evans Warncee Robinson LLC
6075 Barfield Road, Suite 1000
Atlanta, Georgia 30328
404-841-9400, Extension 43
Toll Free: (888) 229-2407
www.evansinjurylaw.com
w.evans@ewrlawfirm.com
m.forster@ewrlawfirm.com

FutureMVP
First Concourse Parkway, Suite 800
Atlanta, Georgia 30328
info@futuremvp.org
(470) 506-1263
Founder: Masdesta "MJ" Jackson
We secure your child's future through sports safety before they play.

Northpoint Roofing Systems
102 Springfield Center Drive
Woodstock, Georgia 30188
(678) 345-1711
www.northpointroofingsystems.com

Mrs. Lovetta Coker
Global Refuge Ministries
5563 Memorial Drive
Stone Mountain, GA 30083
Pastor Alfred Lansana
Dawn Nimer Thomas

Dawn Thomas
Originally from Opelousas, Louisiana, and now residing in Bethlehem, Georgia. She is actively involved in her home churches, participating in leadership and intercessory prayer.

White Oak Springs Missionary Baptist Church
123 E. New Street
Winder, GA 30097
(770) 867-6531
www.wosembc.com
Pastor Nathaniel Moultrie
First Lady Carla Moultrie

Pastor Kerney Thomas
Life Church Carencro
P.O. Box 145, Carencro, Louisiana 70520
(856) 777-7715
www.kerneythomas.org

Anthony's and Son Automotive Repair
1868 Candler Road
Decatur, Georgia 30032
(404) 284-9888

Ms. Kim Wood of Atlanta, Georgia

Jermail "Skoop" Hayes
VinylCutMaxx@gmail.com
#labeleverything

Ronnie J. Wells Publishing
adonai314@yahoo.com

A Journey of Transformation

☙❧

Someone once asked me if my book could save lives. The answer is "yes". I am incredibly grateful to you for taking the time to read it.

I have two small requests:

1. Share Your Testimony. Please consider writing a review to let others know how this book has impacted your life.

2. Encourage Sharing. If you can, encourage two of your friends to purchase the book. If they're unable to, consider buying it for them and ask them to pass it forward.

This book offers a new journey filled with fulfillment - a lifetime adventure.

Chapter 1

ಅ೩೮ಾ

"Unveiling the Seven 'I Am' Statements of Jesus." Discovering Yourself in the Identity of Jesus.

JESUS WHO AM: Am I asking Jesus who I am or is Jesus telling me who He is?

Revealed: The Profound Meaning Behind Jesus' Seven 'I Am' Declarations

1. "I am the bread of life." John 6:35
2. "I am the light of the world." John 8:12
3. "I am the gate for the sheep." John 10:7
4. "I am the good shepherd." John 10:11
5. "I am the resurrection and the life." John 11:25
6. "I am the way, the truth, and the life." John 14:6
7. "I am the true vine." John 15:1

JESUS WHO AM:
Am I asking Jesus who I am or is Jesus telling me who He is?

Matthew 16:13-14

"When Jesus came to the region of Caesarea Philippi, he asked His disciples, "Who do people say the Son of Man is?" They replied, "Some say John the Baptist; others say Elijah; and still others, Jeremiah or one of the prophets."

Revealed:
The Profound Meaning Behind Jesus' Seven 'I Am' Declarations

The "I am" statements of Jesus in the Bible define His character, purpose, and reason for being. They reveal His identity as the Son of God and convey His divine power and authority.

1. **"I am the bread of life." (John 6:35).** Jesus is the sustainer of spiritual life, providing nourishment and satisfaction to those who believe in Him.

2. **"I am the light of the world." (John 8:12).** Jesus is the source of spiritual enlightenment, guiding people out of darkness and into the truth.

3. **"I am the door." (John 10:9).** Jesus is the only way to access salvation and enter into a relationship with God.

4. **"I am the good shepherd." (John 10:11).** Jesus is the caring and protective leader who lies down His life for His sheep, symbolizing His sacrifice for humanity.

5. **"I am the resurrection and the life." (John 11:25).** Jesus has power over death and offers eternal life to those who believe in Him.

6. **"I am the way, the truth, and the life." (John 14:6).** Jesus is the exclusive path to God, the ultimate truth, and the source of abundant life.

7. **"I am the true vine." (John 15:1).** Jesus is the source of spiritual nourishment and sustenance, and believers are branches that must remain connected to Him to bear fruit.

These "I am" statements convey the divinity of Jesus, His role as the Messiah, and the fulfillment of Old Testament prophecies. They provide us with a deeper understanding of His character, purpose, and reason for being.

1. Jesus said, "I am the bread of life." Nourishment for the Soul

My Dearest Beloved,

I am writing to you today to shed light on why I am often referred to as the bread of life. This title holds great depth and significance, for it goes beyond the physical sustenance that bread provides and delves into the spiritual nourishment that I offer to all who seek me.

First and foremost, bread is a fundamental source of sustenance, providing nourishment and sustaining life. In the same way, I am the source of spiritual nourishment that is essential for the sustenance of the soul. Just as bread sustains the physical body, I offer sustenance to the spirit, providing the strength and nourishment needed to navigate the challenges of life.

Moreover, bread is a 'staple food' that is accessible to all, regardless of social status or background. Similarly, I am accessible to all who seek me, without discrimination or judgment. I offer myself freely to anyone who is in need, and my love and grace are available to all who come to me.

Furthermore, bread is a symbol of unity and community. When people gather to share a meal, bread often takes center stage, symbolizing unity and fellowship. In the same way, I bring people together in a community of faith and love. I am the unifying force that binds my followers together in a shared journey of faith, hope, and love.

Additionally, bread is a symbol of my sacrificial nature. Just as bread is made through the process of grinding wheat and baking, I underwent a sacrificial process through my suffering and death on the cross. My body was broken like bread, and my blood was shed as a symbol of the ultimate sacrifice for the redemption of humanity.

Moreover, just as bread provides daily sustenance, I offer myself as the daily source of spiritual sustenance. I am the sustainer of life, providing the strength and nourishment needed to face each day's challenges and opportunities. Those who partake of me will never hunger or thirst spiritually, for I am the fulfillment of all spiritual needs.

In conclusion, I am the bread of life because I am the source of spiritual nourishment, accessible to all, unifying communities, symbolizing sacrifice, and providing daily sustenance to the soul. I invite you to partake of me, to experience the fullness of life and the richness of spiritual nourishment that I offer.

With all-encompassing love,
Jesus

Aspiration

- "I am the bread of life, offering spiritual nourishment to all who seek sustenance for their souls."

- "I am the bread of life, accessible to all, without discrimination, offering my love and grace freely to those in need."

- "I am the bread of life, unifying communities in a shared journey of faith, hope, and love."

- "I am the bread of life, symbolizing my sacrificial nature, offering myself as the ultimate sacrifice for the redemption of humanity."

- "I am the bread of life, providing daily sustenance to the soul, fulfilling all spiritual needs and offering strength to face life's challenges."

Affirmation

- "I affirm that Jesus is the bread of life, nourishing my spirit and providing sustenance in times of need."

- "I embrace the truth that Jesus, as the bread of life, is accessible to all, offering love and grace without reservation."

- "I am grateful for the unity and fellowship found in Jesus, the bread of life, as He brings us together in a community of faith and love."

- "I find comfort in the sacrificial love of Jesus, the bread of life, knowing that His ultimate sacrifice brings redemption and salvation."

- "I affirm that Jesus, as the bread of life, is my daily sustenance, providing strength and fulfilling all my spiritual needs as I navigate life's journey."

Meaning

When Jesus proclaimed, "I am the bread of life," He was conveying profound and multifaceted symbolism that holds deep spiritual significance. This declaration is found in the Gospel of John, where Jesus uses powerful metaphors to convey essential truths about His nature and the spiritual sustenance that He offers to those who follow Him.

1. Spiritual Nourishment. By referring to Himself as the bread of life, Jesus emphasizes that He is the ultimate source of spiritual nourishment. Just as bread sustains the physical body, Jesus provides sustenance for the soul. He offers eternal nourishment and fulfillment that transcends temporal desires and provides enduring spiritual satisfaction.

2. Accessibility and Inclusivity. Jesus, as the bread of life, signifies accessibility and inclusivity. Bread is a fundamental food that transcends social barriers, and in the same way, Jesus is accessible to all who seek Him. His love, grace, and salvation are available to everyone, without discrimination or exclusion. This declaration underscores the universal and unconditional nature of His offer of spiritual sustenance.

3. Unity and Community. Bread often symbolizes unity and community, especially in the context of shared meals and fellowship. By identifying Himself as the bread of life, Jesus highlights His role in unifying His followers and creating a community of faith and love. Through Him, believers are brought together in a shared journey of spiritual growth, mutual support, and shared purpose.

4. Sacrificial Nature. Jesus' proclamation as the bread of life also reflects His sacrificial nature. Bread is made through a process of grinding wheat and baking, and in a similar vein, Jesus underwent suffering and sacrifice for the redemption of humanity. His body, broken like bread, and His blood shed on the cross, serve as a symbol of His ultimate sacrifice for the salvation and spiritual nourishment of humanity.

5. Daily Sustenance and Fulfillment. The metaphor of Jesus as the bread of life signifies that He is the sustainer of life, providing the essential spiritual nourishment needed for daily living. Believers find in Jesus the fulfillment of their deepest spiritual needs, and His presence offers the strength, sustenance, and guidance necessary to navigate life's challenges and triumphs.

Ultimately, when Jesus proclaims, "I am the bread of life," He invites people to partake in a deeper spiritual understanding of His identity and the transformative nature of the sustenance He offers. This profound declaration encompasses the provision of spiritual nourishment, accessibility to all, unity in community, sacrificial love, and daily sustenance, presenting a rich tapestry of spiritual truths and promises for those who seek to follow Him.

Bible Verses
Jesus saying, "I am the bread of life."

1. John 6:35 (NIV). "Then Jesus declared, 'I am the bread of life. Whoever comes to me will never go hungry, and whoever believes in me will never be thirsty.'"

2. John 6:48 (NIV). "I am the bread of life. Your ancestors ate the manna in the wilderness, yet they died."

3. **John 6:51 (NIV).** "I am the living bread that came down from heaven. Whoever eats this bread will live forever. This bread is my flesh, which I will give for the life of the world."

4. **John 6:58 (NIV).** "This is the bread that came down from heaven. Your ancestors ate manna and died, but whoever feeds on this bread will live forever."

These verses from the Gospel of John capture the profound significance of Jesus as the bread of life and emphasize the everlasting sustenance and spiritual nourishment that He provides to those who come to Him in faith.

2. Jesus said, "I am the light of the world." Illuminating Truth and Grace

My dear beloved followers,

I am writing to you today to elaborate on the profound truth that I have shared with you: "I am the light of the world." These words carry deep significance and offer insight into the very essence of my mission, purpose, and the evidence of my divinity.

In proclaiming, "I am the light of the world," I seek to convey several foundational truths that reflect the divine nature of my being and the transformative impact of my presence in your lives and in the world at large.

Firstly, light represents truth, guidance, and clarity. In calling myself "the light of the world," I am emphasizing that

I am the ultimate source of spiritual truth and guidance. My teachings and presence illuminate the path to understanding, righteousness, and salvation. In a world overshadowed by darkness; the darkness of sin, suffering, and spiritual blindness. I offer the radiant light of divine truth, which leads to eternal life and fulfillment.

Moreover, light dispels darkness, symbolizing the triumph of good over evil. By identifying as the light of the world, I signify my role in overcoming the darkness of sin, ignorance, and despair. My presence brings hope, healing, and deliverance, dispelling the shadows of fear and offering the promise of redemption to all who embrace me.

Furthermore, light brings warmth, comfort, and life. As the light of the world, I bring warmth and healing to the human soul, offering solace to the brokenhearted and renewal to the weary. My light brings life to the spiritually dead, reviving hearts and spirits with the transformative power of love, grace, and divine presence.

The evidence of my identity as the light of the world is abundantly clear in my words, actions, and the witness of those who have encountered me. My teachings illuminate the path to righteousness, love, and reconciliation, guiding you towards a life of purpose and fulfillment. My miraculous works and deeds serve as a radiant testimony to my divine nature, demonstrating my authority over physical and spiritual realms and revealing the boundless compassion and power of the heavenly Father.

Furthermore, by reflecting my light through your own lives, you become beacons of hope and truth in a world shrouded in darkness. As my followers, you carry the responsibility and privilege of illuminating the world with the light of love, compassion, and righteousness, thereby bearing witness to the transformative power of my presence in your lives.

In understanding the significance of my declaration as the light of the world, you gain insight into the fundamental nature of our relationship and the transformative impact of my presence in your lives. Embrace my light, walk in the radiance of my truth, and allow the brilliance of my love to shine through you, illuminating the world with the divine light of hope and salvation.

May you continue to walk in the light, and may your lives be a testimony to the transformative power of my presence in the world.

With boundless love and grace,
Jesus

Aspiration

- Jesus is the ultimate source of spiritual truth and guidance, illuminating the path to understanding, righteousness, and salvation.

- By identifying as the light of the world, Jesus signifies His role in overcoming the darkness of sin, ignorance, and despair, bringing hope, healing, and deliverance to all who embrace Him.

- Jesus brings warmth and comfort to the human soul, offering solace to the brokenhearted and renewal to the weary, and reviving hearts and spirits with the transformative power of love, grace, and divine presence.

- The evidence of Jesus's identity as the light of the world is abundantly clear in His teachings, miraculous works, and the witness of those who have encountered Him, demonstrating His authority over physical and spiritual realms and revealing the boundless compassion and power of the heavenly Father.

- By reflecting Jesus's light through their own lives, His followers become beacons of hope and truth in a world shrouded in darkness, illuminating the world with the light of love, compassion, and righteousness.

Affirmation

- "I embrace the illuminating presence of Jesus as the light of the world, guiding me towards spiritual truth and leading me on a path of righteousness and grace."

- "Jesus, as the light of the world, dispels the darkness of doubt and fear in my life, infusing me with hope, courage, and unwavering faith."

- "I bask in the warmth of Jesus's light, finding solace and renewal in His comforting presence, and allowing His love to heal and revive my weary soul."

- "The radiant evidence of Jesus being the light of the world is abundantly clear in His teachings and transformative power, inspiring me to reflect His love and compassion in all my interactions."

- "As a beacon of the light of Jesus, I strive to shine brightly, illuminating the world with hope, kindness, and unwavering faith, spreading the radiance of His love to all those around me."

Meaning

When Jesus proclaimed, "I am the light of the world," it was a profound declaration of His divine role and the transformative influence He brings to humanity. In making this statement, Jesus was conveying several significant meanings:

1. Spiritual Illumination. By identifying Himself as the light of the world, Jesus was emphasizing His role as the ultimate source of spiritual truth and enlightenment. In a world shrouded in darkness, sin, and spiritual blindness, Jesus offers the light of wisdom, understanding, and guidance, illuminating the path to righteousness, salvation, and the knowledge of God's kingdom.

2. Overcoming Darkness. As the light of the world, Jesus signifies His ability to overcome the pervasive darkness of sin, ignorance, and despair. His presence and teachings dispel spiritual obscurity, offering hope, healing, and deliverance to all who embrace Him. In doing so, He brings clarity, purpose, and transformation into the lives of those who are lost in the shadows of a broken world.

3. Revelation of Truth and Love. Jesus as the light of the world reveals the nature of God's love, compassion, and grace to humanity. His life, teachings, and sacrificial death demonstrate the selfless and unwavering love that God has for humanity, illuminating the path to reconciliation, forgiveness, and eternal life. Through His example, Jesus shows the transformative power of love and the divine purpose for human existence.

4. Authority and Divine Presence. The declaration, "I am the light of the world" asserts Jesus's authority over spiritual and cosmic realms, as well as His identity as the Son of God. It signifies His unique and unparalleled role in bringing God's divine presence into the world, bringing the radiance of the heavenly Father's love, truth, and righteousness to humanity.

5. Call to Reflect and Shine. Jesus's proclamation challenges His followers to reflect His light in their own lives, becoming beacons of hope, love, and truth in a world immersed in spiritual darkness. By embodying His teachings and sharing His love with others, His followers become agents of divine illumination, spreading the radiance of His message to all corners of the earth.

In conclusion, when Jesus declared, "I am the light of the world," He was communicating His role as the source of spiritual enlightenment, hope, and transformation for humanity. His proclamation resonates with deep theological significance, offering guidance, comfort, and a pathway to reconciliation with God and one another. It calls individuals to embrace the light of His teachings, to stand against darkness, and to reflect His illuminating love and truth in their own lives.

Bible Verses
Jesus saying, "I am the light of the world."

1. John 8:12 (NIV). "When Jesus spoke again to the people, he said, 'I am the light of the world. Whoever follows me will never walk in darkness but will have the light of life.'"

2. John 9:5 (NIV). "While I am in the world, I am the light of the world."

3. Matthew 5:14 (NIV). "You are the light of the world. A town built on a hill cannot be hidden."

4. Luke 2:32 (NIV). "A light for revelation to the Gentiles, and the glory of your people Israel."

5. John 12:46 (NIV). "I have come into the world as a light so that no one who believes in me should stay in darkness."

These verses from the books of John, Matthew, and Luke emphasize Jesus's role as the light of the world, offering spiritual guidance, enlightenment, and hope to all who embrace His teachings and follow His path.

3. Jesus said, "I am the gate for the sheep."
Welcoming All to the Flock

My dear disciples,

I write to you today to offer guidance and understanding with regard to my statement, "I am the gate for the sheep." This symbolism is filled with deep spiritual meaning and serves as an assurance of my role and purpose in your lives.

Firstly, the image of a gate is evocative of protection and safety. In ancient times, the gate of a sheepfold was the only entrance and exit. It was the place where the shepherd would lead the sheep in and out of the safety of the fold. By proclaiming that I am the gate for the sheep, I am conveying that I am the sole means through which you, my followers, can experience true protection and security. Just as a gate shields the sheep from harm, I am the source of refuge and sanctuary for all who seek me.

Furthermore, the gate signifies control and authority. Only the shepherd had the authority to open and close the gate, deciding who enters and who goes out. In this way, I, as the gate, undertake the responsibility of guiding and leading my flock. I am the authority that determines the course of your lives, offering direction and purpose. Through me, you find the pathway to righteousness and fulfillment.

Moreover, as the gate for the sheep, I am the point of access to abundant life. The pasture lies beyond the gate, providing sustenance, nourishment, and growth. By aligning myself with the gate, I am emphasizing that through our relationship, you will find not only safety and protection, but also the fullness of life. It is through me that you will experience the richness of spiritual nourishment and the promise of eternal life.

Additionally, the reference to "the sheep" exemplifies the nature of our relationship. In ancient shepherd-and-sheep allegories, the sheep represent believers and followers. By identifying you as my sheep, I am acknowledging the intimate connection between us. Just as a shepherd knows His sheep, so too do I know you intimately and personally. I am attuned to your needs, concerns, and desires, and I am wholly committed to caring for and leading you.

The significance of this statement, "I am the gate for the sheep," goes beyond mere metaphor. It encapsulates the essence of who I am and the purpose I fulfill. I am your guardian, providing security and shielding you from harm. I am your leader, directing and guiding your paths. I am your sustenance, offering the abundance of life, both in the present and for eternity. Moreover, I am intimately connected to each of you, knowing you individually, and caring for you unconditionally.

In embracing the role of the gate, I am proclaiming my divinity and the unique relationship I share with my followers. Through me, you find protection, guidance, and fullness of life. It is through me that you enter into the blessings of the Kingdom and experience the depth of my love and care for you.

As your shepherd and gate, I urge you to dwell in the assurance that I am ever-present, ever watchful, and ever leading. Trust in me, for I am the gate for the sheep, and through my love and guidance, you will find true fulfillment and eternal joy.

With unwavering love and steadfast devotion, Jesus

Aspiration

- Jesus as the gate symbolizes His role as the sole pathway to spiritual protection and security.

- In proclaiming Himself as the gate, Jesus establishes His authority as the guiding figure for His followers, providing direction and purpose in their lives.

- "I am the gate for the sheep" signifies Jesus as the gateway to abundant life, offering nourishment and sustenance to those who follow Him.

- This statement reflects the intimate connection between Jesus and His followers, emphasizing His personal care and knowledge of each individual.

- As the gate for the sheep, Jesus embodies the essence of divine love and guidance, leading His followers into the blessings of the Kingdom and eternal life.

Affirmation

- "Through Jesus, I find protection and safety, for He is the gate for the sheep, watching over and shielding me from harm."

- "In Jesus, I discover purpose and direction, for He is the gate leading me on the path of righteousness and fulfillment."

- "Jesus is the gateway to abundant life, and through Him, I am nourished and sustained, experiencing the fullness of spiritual blessings."

- "As one of Jesus' sheep, I find comfort in the knowledge that He knows me intimately, caring for me with unwavering love and understanding."

- "In recognizing Jesus as the gate for the sheep, I embrace His divine guidance and experience the joy of dwelling in His presence, secure in His love and care."

Meaning

When Jesus declared, "I am the gate for the sheep," He conveyed several powerful meanings:

1. Protection and Security. By identifying Himself as the gate, Jesus symbolized His role as the sole source of protection and safety for His followers. The image of a gate evokes a sense of security, indicating that through Him, believers find refuge from harm and danger.

2. Guidance and Direction. As the gate, Jesus signifies His authority as the ultimate guide for His followers, leading them on the path of righteousness and offering a sense of purpose and direction in their lives.

3. Nourishment and Abundance. Jesus, as the gate for the sheep, represents the gateway to spiritual nourishment and abundance. Through Him, believers access the sustenance and fulfillment that their souls crave, experiencing the richness of spiritual blessings and abundant life.

4. Intimate Care and Knowledge. By proclaiming Himself as the gate for the sheep, Jesus emphasizes His personal care and intimate knowledge of each individual. This intimate connection assures believers that they are not just part of a collective flock, but that Jesus knows them individually and cares deeply for their well-being.

5. Divine Love and Guidance. Jesus' words reveal His role as the embodiment of divine love and guidance. As the gate for the sheep, He leads His followers into the blessings of the Kingdom and eternal life, offering them the assurance of a loving shepherd who watches over and cares for His flock.

Overall, the intent of Jesus' words, "I am the gate for the sheep", is to convey His exclusive role as the source of protection, guidance, nourishment, and love for those who choose to follow Him. It emphasizes the intimate and caring nature of His relationship with His followers, assuring them of His constant presence and unwavering commitment to their spiritual well-being.

Bible Verses
Jesus said, "I am the gate for the sheep."

1. John 10:7. "Therefore Jesus said again, 'Very truly I tell you, I am the gate for the sheep.'"

2. John 10:9. "I am the gate; whoever enters through me will be saved. They will come in and go out, and find pasture."

3. John 10:1. "Very truly I tell you Pharisees, anyone who does not enter the sheep pen by the gate, but climbs in by some other way, is a thief and a robber."

4. John 10:2. "The one who enters by the gate is the shepherd of the sheep."

5. John 10:11. "I am the good shepherd. The good shepherd lays down His life for the sheep."

These verses from the book of John in the Bible emphasize Jesus' role as the gate for the sheep, highlighting His provision of salvation, protection, and guidance for those who follow Him.

4. Jesus said, "I am the Good Shepherd." Guiding and Protecting His Flock.

Dear Beloved Followers,

As I address you, I want to emphasize and elaborate on the significance of the statement, "I am the Good Shepherd." This declaration holds profound meaning and reflects the intent, purpose, and attitude that define the role of the Good Shepherd.

1. Meaning of being the Good Shepherd

In proclaiming, "I am the Good Shepherd," I seek to convey the depth of my care and devotion to each one of you. A shepherd leads, protects, nourishes, and guides the flock with unwavering love and attention. As the Good Shepherd, I take on the responsibility of nurturing and safeguarding each of you, knowing you by name and tending to your individual needs with compassion and understanding.

2. Intent of being the Good Shepherd

My intent as the Good Shepherd is to offer you a sense of security, belonging, and purpose. I aim to lead you along the paths of righteousness, providing you with spiritual nourishment, protection from harm, and guidance towards abundant life. Through this declaration, I underscore the depth of my commitment to each of you, ensuring that no one is lost or forgotten under my care.

3. Purpose of being the Good Shepherd

As the Good Shepherd, my purpose is to lay down my life for the sheep, epitomizing sacrificial love and unwavering dedication. I strive to protect you from all harm, to comfort you in times of distress, and to shepherd you towards the fulfillment of your spiritual journey. My purpose is to bring unity, peace, and abundance to the flock, ensuring that each of you experiences the fullness of life that I have come to offer.

4. Attitude of being the Good Shepherd

The attitude of the Good Shepherd is one of selflessness, humility, and love. I approach my role with a heart full of compassion, readily tending to the needs of the flock, and rejoicing in the presence of each and every one of you. My attitude reflects a deep sense of responsibility, gentleness, and protection, ensuring that every sheep is cared for, sheltered, and guided with tenderness and patience.

In conclusion, the declaration, "I am the Good Shepherd", encapsulates the deep love, care, and commitment that I have for each of you. It reflects my earnest desire to provide you with security, guidance, and abundance, while exemplifying the sacrificial love that defines my relationship with you. Rest assured that as the Good Shepherd, I am always present, always vigilant, and always ready to lead you into the fullness of life.

With Love,
Jesus

Aspiration

- "I aspire to lead others with compassion and understanding, seeking to guide them towards spiritual nourishment and fulfillment, just as Jesus proclaimed, 'I am the Good Shepherd.'

- "Inspired by the selfless love of the Good Shepherd, I aspire to care for those in my charge with humility, offering them protection, comfort, and unity in their spiritual journey."

- "In aspiring to emulate the attitude of the Good Shepherd, I strive to shepherd others with unwavering dedication, ensuring that each individual feels known, valued, and guided towards abundant life."

- "Echoing the intent of the Good Shepherd, I aspire to lay down my life in service of others, exemplifying sacrificial love and a steadfast commitment to their well-being and spiritual growth."

- "I aspire to embody the purpose of the Good Shepherd, leading others along the paths of righteousness, fostering peace, and shepherding them towards unity and the fullness of life that Jesus promised as the Good Shepherd."

These statements reflect aspirations grounded in the principles and qualities of the Good Shepherd as articulated by Jesus, encapsulating a desire to emulate His selfless love, guidance, protection, and sacrificial commitment in shepherding others.

Affirmation

- "I affirm the profound love and care of Jesus, who declared, 'I am the Good Shepherd', assuring me of His unwavering commitment to lead, protect, and guide me through life's journey."

- "I affirm my trust in Jesus as the Good Shepherd, knowing that He knows me by name, tends to my needs, and leads me towards spiritual nourishment and abundance."

- "I affirm the reassurance of Jesus' words, 'I am the Good Shepherd', finding comfort in His steadfast presence, His willingness to lay down His life for me, and His tender guidance along righteous paths."

- "I affirm my sense of belonging and security in Jesus, the Good Shepherd, who gathers me into His flock, ensuring that I am known, valued, and safeguarded under His loving care."

- "I affirm my gratitude for the sacrificial love of Jesus, the Good Shepherd, who selflessly tends to my well-being, protects me from harm, and leads me towards the fullness of life promised in His declaration: 'I am the Good Shepherd.'"

These affirmations reflect a deep sense of trust, gratitude, and reassurance in the love and guidance of Jesus as the Good Shepherd, offering comfort, security, and a profound sense of belonging to those who affirm these truths.

Meaning

When Jesus declared, "I am the Good Shepherd," He used a metaphor that carries profound meaning and implications. The concept of a shepherd was familiar to Jesus' audience, especially in the agricultural and pastoral context of ancient Israel. Here are some key meanings behind Jesus' assertion:

1. Protection and Care. By referencing Himself as the Good Shepherd, Jesus conveyed His role as a caretaker and protector of His followers. In the same way that a shepherd guards and cares for His flock, Jesus ensures the well-being and safety of those who belong to Him.

2. Personal Relationship. The imagery of a shepherd underscores the intimate and personal nature of the relationship between Jesus and His followers. Just as a shepherd knows each of His sheep by name, Jesus knows and cares for each of His followers individually.

3. Guidance and Direction. A shepherd leads His flock to green pastures and still waters, providing sustenance and guidance. In a similar manner, Jesus offers spiritual nourishment, guidance, and direction to His followers, leading them towards abundant life and fulfillment.

4. Sacrificial Love. The designation of "Good Shepherd" also points to Jesus's sacrificial love. A good shepherd is willing to lay down His life for the sheep, and Jesus emphasizes this sacrificial aspect in His role as the ultimate shepherd who gives His life for the salvation of His people.

5. Unity and Community. The shepherd metaphor exemplifies the unity and community within the flock. Jesus, as the Good Shepherd, unites His followers into one flock, fostering a sense of belonging and unity among believers.

When Jesus proclaimed, "I am the Good Shepherd," He conveyed a message of reassurance, love, protection, and self-sacrifice. This declaration encapsulates the depth of His care for His followers, the intimacy of His relationship with them, and His commitment to guiding them towards spiritual flourishing and unity within the community of believers.

Bible Verses
Jesus declaring, "I am the Good Shepherd."

1. John 10:11 (NIV). "I am the good shepherd. The good shepherd lays down His life for the sheep."

2. John 10:14 (NIV). "I am the good shepherd; I know my sheep and my sheep know me."

3. John 10:27 (NIV). "My sheep listen to my voice; I know them, and they follow me."

4. Hebrews 13:20 (NIV). "Now may the God of peace, who through the blood of the eternal covenant brought back from the dead our Lord Jesus, that great Shepherd of the sheep…"

5. **1 Peter 2:25 (NIV).** "For you were like sheep going astray, but now you have returned to the Shepherd and Overseer of your souls."

These verses from the New Testament highlight Jesus' assertion of being the Good Shepherd, emphasizing His sacrificial love, intimate knowledge of His followers, and the guidance and care He provides to those who belong to him.

5. Jesus said, "I am the resurrection and the life." Hope Beyond Death.

My beloved child,

I write to you today with a heart overflowing with love and a desire to illuminate the depth of my being as the resurrection and the life. It is my earnest hope that in these words, you may discover the profound significance of my purpose, the evidence of who I am, and the multifaceted facets of my identity.

First and foremost, as the resurrection and the life, I embody the promise and the fulfillment of eternal life. My purpose transcends earthly existence, for I came to offer a pathway to everlasting life and restoration. The profound truth is that in me, death is not the end, but a transition into the fullness of life with the Father.

The evidence of my identity as the resurrection and the life is resplendent in the miracles I performed during my earthly ministry. From the raising of Lazarus from the dead to my own triumphant resurrection, these were manifestations of my divine authority over life and death. They serve as testimonies to the veracity of my claim and the assurance that through belief in me, you too shall experience eternal life.

Furthermore, in declaring, "I am the resurrection and the life," I encapsulate the essence of who I am. I am the embodiment of hope, the conqueror of sin and death, and the source of abundant, eternal life. My identity is intricately intertwined with the concept of resurrection not only as a future event but also as a present reality that infuses your everyday life with purpose, meaning, and joy.

As the resurrection and the life, I invite you to partake in a profound and transformative relationship with me. I beckon you to embrace the truth that is in me; you find not only eternal life but also the fullness of life here and now. Through me, you are called to live with unwavering hope, bold faith, and an abiding sense of purpose.

My beloved, as the resurrection and the life, I extend to you the gift of my presence, my love, and the assurance that nothing, not even death itself, can separate you from the boundless love and life I offer. I am the fulfillment of the deepest longings of your heart, the harbinger of new beginnings, and the beacon of eternal hope.

May these words resonate in the depths of your soul, offering solace, assurance, and a renewed understanding of the profound significance of my identity as the resurrection and the life. May you walk in the radiance of my love, firmly grounded in the unwavering truth of who I am and the promise of eternal life that I freely bestow upon you.

With unending love, Your Savior and Redeemer

Aspiration

- Through Jesus, I find the assurance that my life is eternally secured in the promise of resurrection and the fullness of life beyond this earthly existence.
- In embracing Jesus as the resurrection and the life, I am empowered to live each day with unwavering hope, knowing that in Him, all things are made new, and all obstacles are overcome.

- Jesus' proclamation as the resurrection and the life beckons me to walk boldly in faith, unshackled by the fear of death, and confident in the transformative power of His love and grace.

- As I grasp the profound truth of Jesus' identity as the resurrection and the life, I am emboldened to live a purpose-driven life, rooted in the surety of an eternal destiny and the abundant life He offers.

- With Jesus as the resurrection and the life, I am afforded the gift of embracing each day with gratitude, knowing that even in the face of challenges, His presence ensures that my life is suffused with significance, purpose, and the hope of eternal joy.

Affirmation

- I affirm that through Jesus, I am assured of the promise of eternal life, transcending the limitations of this world and embracing the fullness of existence in the presence of the Divine.

- I affirm the transformative truth that in Jesus, the concept of resurrection extends beyond a future hope, infusing my present life with purpose, hope, and the assurance of a meaningful, everlasting existence.

- I affirm my unwavering faith in Jesus as the resurrection and the life, understanding that through Him, I am liberated from the fear of death and empowered to live boldly, embracing each moment with hope and joy.

- I affirm Jesus as the cornerstone of my faith, recognizing that in Him, I find the source of eternal life, the embodiment of enduring love, and the promise of a future beyond earthly constraints.

- I affirm the profound impact of Jesus' declaration as the resurrection and the life, knowing that in Him, I find solace, purpose, and the inexhaustible wellspring of hope that sustains me through all seasons of life.

Meaning

When Jesus declared, "I am the resurrection and the life," He was conveying profound spiritual truths about His identity and the nature of faith. This statement holds rich significance, encompassing both the assurance of eternal life and the transformative power of His presence.

1. Assurance of Eternal Life. In proclaiming Himself as "the resurrection," Jesus communicated that through belief in Him, individuals are not only promised eternal life after earthly death but are also invited to experience the reality of this eternal life in the present. He serves as the embodiment of hope beyond the temporal constraints of human existence.

2. Triumph over Death. Jesus' assertion as "the resurrection" signifies His victory over death, offering believers the reassurance that through faith in Him, the fear of mortality is overcome. He provides solace to those grieving and instills a sense of peace, assuring that the essence of life transcends physical boundaries.

3. Source of Abundant Life. By proclaiming "I am the life," Jesus highlights His role as the source and sustainer of all life. He extends an invitation to partake in a life imbued with purpose, meaning, and fulfillment, transcending mere existence. Through Him, believers are invited to live fully, embracing the richness of a life anchored in His teachings and abundant grace.

4. Relationship with Christ. Jesus' declaration underscores the intimate relationship He offers to those who believe in Him, emphasizing the interconnectedness between Himself as the source of life and those who embrace His teachings. His words invite individuals to commune with Him, finding vitality and spiritual nourishment in His presence.

5. Transformation and New Beginnings. Jesus as "the resurrection and the life" signifies the transformative power of His words and deeds. He evokes hope, restoration, and renewal, assuring believers that in Him, they find the capacity for spiritual rebirth and an opportunity to live authentically with purpose and vitality.

In essence, Jesus' profound statement encapsulates the spiritual truths of transcendent life, freedom from the fear of death, and the invitation to a transformative relationship with Him. It encompasses the promise of eternal life and the call to embrace the fullness of life in His presence, offering hope, purpose, and renewal to all who believe in Him.

Bible Verses
Declaration of Jesus, "I am the resurrection and the life."

1. John 11:25-26 (NIV). "Jesus said to her, I am the resurrection and the life. The one who believes in me will live, even though they die; and whoever lives by believing in me will never die. Do you believe this?"

2. 1 Corinthians 15:22 (NIV). "For as in Adam all die, so in Christ all will be made alive."

3. Romans 6:5 (NIV). "For if we have been united with him in a death like His, we will certainly also be united with him in a resurrection like His."

4. 1 Peter 1:3 (NIV). "Praise be to the God and Father of our Lord Jesus Christ! In His great mercy he has given us new birth into a living hope through the resurrection of Jesus Christ from the dead."

5. Colossians 3:1-4 (NIV). "Since, then, you have been raised with Christ, set your hearts on things above, where Christ is, seated at the right hand of God. Set your minds on things above, not on earthly things. For you died, and your life is now hidden with Christ in God. When Christ, who is your life, appears, then you also will appear with him in glory."

These verses from the New Testament underscore the pivotal role of Jesus as the source of resurrection and life, offering believers the promise of eternal life, spiritual union with Christ, and the transformative power of His resurrection.

6. Jesus said, "I am the way the truth and the life." Pathway to Redemption

My Dearest Beloved,

I write to you with the deepest love and compassion, as I yearn for your hearts to truly comprehend the profound truth of my divine purpose and the extraordinary power vested in my declaration, "I am the way, the truth, and the life."

As I reflect upon these words, I am profoundly moved by the significance they hold for those who seek solace, guidance, and ultimate fulfillment in their lives. Allow me to unveil the transcendent power encapsulated within this declaration, a power that flows from the very essence of my divinity and purpose.

First and foremost, in proclaiming, "I am the way," I unveil the path to eternal salvation and communion with the Father. I am the embodiment of the divine roadmap leading humanity to the profound truth of spiritual reconciliation and everlasting peace. Through me, you will find the way to the Father, for I am the conduit through which divine grace is bestowed upon all who seek to follow in my footsteps.

In declaring, "I am the truth," I illuminate the essence of divine revelation and uncompromising authenticity. Every word I speak resonates with the intrinsic truth that emanates from the heart of the Father. Embracing my teachings and embodying the principles of love, compassion, and righteousness, you will be enfolded in the eternal truths that form the very foundation of the universe.

Moreover, in affirming, "I am the life," I bestow upon you the promise of spiritual vitality, renewal, and enduring significance. Through me, you will discover the deep wellspring of life that transcends the temporal constraints of this world. I impart the essence of abundant life, beckoning you to partake in the fullness of existence and to revel in the eternal communion with the divine.

My beloved, through my divine identity as the way, the truth, and the life, I bear the authority to lead you to the Father, to reveal the unadulterated truth of His love, and to ignite within you the flame of everlasting life. It is through this profound proclamation that my sacred purpose is unveiled, and the omnipotent power of salvation, truth, and eternal life is granted unto humanity.

As you contemplate the depth of my declaration, may your heart be stirred with unwavering faith, resounding hope, and an unyielding commitment to walk in the radiance of my divine light. Embrace the transformative power inherent in knowing me as the way, the truth, and the life, and allow this realization to permeate every facet of your being, guiding you to a life of unparalleled spiritual fulfillment.

With boundless love and unwavering devotion,
Your Savior and Redeemer

Aspiration

- I aspire to walk confidently in the way of love, compassion, and righteousness, knowing that in following Jesus, I am on the path to spiritual fulfillment and communion with the divine.

- I am inspired to seek the unvarnished truth in all aspects of my life, embodying the principles of honesty, integrity, and grace, reflecting the essence of Jesus, who is the embodiment of divine truth.

- I endeavor to embrace each day with a profound sense of purpose and vitality, recognizing that through Jesus, I am the recipient of abundant life, characterized by unwavering hope, enduring joy, and everlasting significance.

- I am steadfast in my commitment to follow Jesus as the way, the truth, and the life, allowing His radiant presence to illuminate my journey and guide me toward a life of ultimate spiritual fulfillment and communion with the Father.

- With a resolute heart, I strive to embody the transformative power of Jesus' declaration, living as a beacon of light, leading others to the way, embodying the truth, and exemplifying a life that bears witness to the everlasting love and grace of our Savior.

Affirmation

- I affirm that Jesus is the guiding way in my life, leading me with love and purpose, illuminating my path with unwavering hope and divine direction.

- I affirm my belief that Jesus embodies the ultimate truth, guiding me to live a life steeped in honesty, compassion, and integrity, reflecting His divine nature.

- I affirm that Jesus is the source of abundant life, infusing my existence with joy, purpose, and everlasting significance, nurturing my soul and spirit with His boundless love and grace.

- I affirm my unwavering trust in Jesus as the way, the truth, and the life, allowing His presence to permeate every aspect of my being, guiding me to a life of unparalleled spiritual fulfillment and communion with the Father.

- I affirm my commitment to emulate Jesus' transformative power by being a beacon of light, leading others to the way, embodying the truth, and sharing a life that testifies to the unending love and grace of our Savior.

Meaning

When Jesus proclaimed, "I am the way, the truth, and the life," He was expressing profound truths about His divinity and the salvation He brings to humanity. Let's unpack the significance of each of these assertions.

"I am the way." By declaring Himself as the way, Jesus was asserting that He is the exclusive path to communion with God. He is the bridge between humanity and the divine, offering reconciliation and access to the Father through His sacrificial death and resurrection.

"I am the truth." Jesus' claim to be the truth signifies that He embodies the unerring and eternal reality of God's nature and purpose. He came to reveal the profound truths of God's love, redemption, and the blueprint for righteous living, guiding humanity into a harmonious relationship with the divine.

"I am the life." In declaring Himself as the life, Jesus speaks to His role as the source of eternal and abundant life. He imparts spiritual vitality, purpose, and everlasting significance to those who follow Him, offering the promise of life beyond the constraints of temporal existence.

Together, these assertions affirm Jesus' exclusive role as the mediator between humanity and God, the embodiment of divine truth, and the bestower of abundant, eternal life to all who believe in Him. Thus, the profound statement "I am the way, the truth, and the life" encompasses Jesus' central role in providing access to God, illuminating the truth, and imparting spiritual vitality and purpose to all who embrace Him.

Bible Verses
Jesus declared, "I am the way, the truth, and the life."

1. John 14:6 (NIV). "Jesus answered, I am the way and the truth and the life. No one comes to the Father except through me."

2. John 10:9 (NIV). "I am the gate; whoever enters through me will be saved. They will come in and go out, and find pasture."

3. 1 Timothy 2:5-6 (NIV). "For there is one God and one mediator between God and mankind, the man Christ Jesus, who gave Himself as a ransom for all people."

4. Colossians 1:15-20 (NIV). "The Son is the image of the invisible God, the firstborn over all creation. For in him all things were created: things in heaven and on earth, visible and invisible, whether thrones or powers or rulers or authorities; all things have been created through him and for him. He is before all things, and in him all things hold together."

5. **Acts 4:12 (NIV).** "Salvation is found in no one else, for there is no other name under heaven given to mankind by which we must be saved."

These verses affirm Jesus' claim to be the exclusive path to salvation, the mediator between God and humanity, and the embodiment of divine truth. They reinforce the foundational significance of Jesus' declaration, "I am the way, the truth, and the life," in the Christian faith.

7. Jesus said, "I am the true Vine."
Bearing Fruit in Abundance

My Beloved Followers,

As I spoke the words, "I am the true Vine," I sought to convey a profound truth rooted in the essence of our intimate connection and interdependence. I implore you to understand the depth of this declaration, for within it lies the very purpose, meaningfulness, and reasoning behind my being the true Vine.

In these words, I intended to illustrate the vital connection between you and me, my dearest branches. I am the true Vine, the ultimate source of nourishment and sustenance for your spiritual growth and vitality. Just as the branches draw sustenance and life from the vine, so must you remain deeply rooted in me, for apart from me, you can do nothing.

I am the embodiment of purpose - a purpose rooted in love, selflessness, and redemption. As the true Vine, I am the conduit through which the lifeblood of divine love flows, infusing you with the strength to bear the fruits of righteousness and grace. Your union with me is essential, for it is through this connection that you find purpose, meaning, and fulfillment.

Furthermore, my declaration as the true Vine is grounded in the profound reasoning of our unity and interconnectedness. Just as the branches are one with the vine, so are you intricately woven into the fabric of my divine design. Your unity with me is a testament to our interconnectedness, signifying that through me, you find your intrinsic value, and through your obedience, you bear the fruit that glorifies our Father.

My dearest ones, to be connected to the true Vine is to partake in the very essence of life and love. It signifies an unbroken communion, a transformative relationship that elevates you to new heights of purpose, fulfillment, and spiritual richness. I am the true Vine, beckoning you to abide in me, allowing my life-giving presence to flow through you and bear fruit that endures.

In closing, as the true Vine, I extend to you an invitation to abide in me with unwavering faith and trust, for in our unity lies the fulfillment of your purpose and the meaningfulness of your existence. Embrace the profound reasoning of our interconnectedness and allow the lifeblood of divine love to flow through you, bearing fruits that reflect our radiant love and grace.

With an abundance of love and unwavering grace,
Your Savior and Redeemer

Aspiration

- I aspire to remain deeply rooted in Jesus, the true Vine, drawing strength and nourishment from His life-giving presence to bear fruit that glorifies God and blesses others.

- I aspire to recognize my interconnectedness with Jesus, the true Vine, understanding that my purpose and meaningfulness are intricately woven into His divine design for my life.

- I aspire to abide in the love and grace of Jesus, the true Vine, allowing His life-giving presence to flow through me, nurturing my spirit and empowering me to reflect His love in all that I do.

- I aspire to cultivate a vibrant and enduring relationship with Jesus, the true Vine, embracing the transformative power of our unity to bring forth fruits of righteousness, kindness, and compassion.

- I aspire to trust in the words of Jesus, the true Vine, reminding myself that apart from Him, I can do nothing, and with Him, I can bear abundant fruits that bless the world and bring glory to God.

Affirmation

- I affirm my connection to Jesus, the true Vine, as I draw spiritual nourishment and strength from His life-giving presence, enabling me to bear fruits of love and compassion.

- I affirm my place in the divine design, recognizing that my purpose and meaningfulness are intertwined with my union with Jesus, the true Vine, and that through Him, I find fulfillment and spiritual abundance.

- I affirm my abidance in the love and grace of Jesus, the true Vine, allowing His transformative presence to flow through me, enriching my heart and soul with His everlasting goodness.

- I affirm my commitment to cultivate a deep and enduring relationship with Jesus, the true Vine, endeavoring to reflect His virtues and character as I grow in unity with Him.

- I affirm my trust in the truth that Jesus, the true Vine, is the source of my strength and vitality, and that through Him, I can bear fruits of righteousness and joy that glorify God and bless humanity.

Meaning

When Jesus declared, "I am the true Vine," He used a powerful metaphor to convey profound spiritual truths to His followers. By likening Himself to a vine, Jesus provided an insightful analogy that communicates essential aspects of the believers' relationship with Him and their spiritual growth. Here are some explanations of what Jesus meant by declaring Himself as the true Vine:

1. Source of Spiritual Nourishment. In calling Himself the true Vine, Jesus emphasized that He is the ultimate source of spiritual nourishment and sustenance for His followers. Like the branches drawing nutrients and water from the vine for their growth and fruit-bearing, believers are to draw their spiritual strength, sustenance, and vitality from their intimate connection with Jesus. He provides the essential nourishment for their spiritual growth, enabling them to thrive and bear good fruit in their lives.

2. Vital Connection and Interdependence. The metaphor of the vine and its branches illustrates the vital connection and interdependence between Jesus and His followers. Just as the branches rely on the vine for their existence, believers are called to remain deeply connected to Jesus, recognizing their dependence on Him for life, purpose, and spiritual abundance. This intimate connection signifies the unity and mutual reliance between Christ and His disciples, underscoring the importance of a profound and enduring relationship.

3. Purpose and Meaningfulness. By identifying Himself as the true Vine, Jesus highlighted the purpose and meaningfulness of the believers' lives through their union with Him. He indicated that the spiritual nourishment derived from abiding in Him is essential for a fruitful and purposeful existence. This declaration invites believers to find their intrinsic value, purpose, and fulfillment in their deep and abiding relationship with Jesus, acknowledging that apart from Him, they can do nothing of lasting significance.

4. Unity and Communion. Furthermore, Jesus' statement as the true Vine underscores the unity and communion between Him and His followers. The interconnectedness of the vine and its branches signifies the intimate and unbroken communion between Christ and His disciples, emphasizing their oneness with Him. Believers are encouraged to embrace this unity, allowing the life-giving presence of Jesus to flow through them and manifest in their lives, bearing fruits that reflect the nature and character of their Savior.

In essence, Jesus' declaration as the true Vine encapsulates the profound truths of spiritual sustenance, vital connection, purpose, meaningfulness, unity, and communion. It invites believers to abide in Him, drawing their strength and vitality from their intimate relationship with Christ, and yielding fruits that glorify God and bless others. This metaphor serves as a poignant reminder of the believers' dependence on Jesus for their spiritual growth, and the transformative power of abiding in His love and grace.

Bible Verses
Jesus' declaration, "I am the true Vine."

1. John 15:5 (NIV). "I am the vine; you are the branches. If you remain in me and I in you, you will bear much fruit; apart from me you can do nothing."

2. John 15:4 (NIV). "Remain in me, as I also remain in you. No branch can bear fruit by itself; it must remain in the vine. Neither can you bear fruit unless you remain in me."

3. John 15:1 (NIV). "I am the true vine, and my Father is the gardener."

4. 1 John 2:6 (NIV). "Whoever claims to live in him must live as Jesus did."

5. Colossians 2:6-7 (NIV). "So then, just as you received Christ Jesus as Lord, continue to live your lives in Him, rooted and built up in Him, strengthened in the faith as you were taught, and overflowing with thankfulness."

These verses demonstrate the significance of abiding in Christ, yielding spiritual fruit, and living in unity with Him. They emphasize the importance of remaining connected to Jesus, the true Vine, for spiritual growth and vitality, as well as the call to reflect His character and live according to His teachings.

Chapter 2

☙❧

Embracing Jesus Seven "I Am" Statement. Jesus the Seven I am

The clarity of Jesus

Jesus Seven I am finding myself in the context of Jesus

Jesus, the Seven I am exclusive to Jesus ONLY

Confession unto Jesus

Dear Friends,

As I have spoken to you, declaring "I am the bread of life, the light of the world, the gate for the sheep, the Good Shepherd, the resurrection and the life, the way, the truth, and the true Vine." I want to convey to you the depth of my purpose, the essence of my being, and the mission I have come to fulfill.

Each of these "I am" statements hold a profound meaning, revealing different facets of my character and purpose. When combined, they form a complete picture of who I am and what I represent to all of humanity.

"I am the bread of life." In this, I am declaring that I am the sustenance for your spiritual needs, the source of nourishment for your soul. I am the one who satisfies the deepest hunger within you and provides eternal sustenance.

"I am the light of the world." I bring illumination to a darkened world, guiding and revealing the path to truth and righteousness. My light dispels darkness, offering hope and guidance to all who seek it.

"I am the gate for the sheep." I am the entry point to the safety and security of the fold. Through me, you find protection, provision, and salvation. I am the way to a restored relationship with our Heavenly Father.

"I am the Good Shepherd." As the Shepherd, I tenderly care for and protect my flock. I lead you, guide you, and am even willing to lay down my life for you, demonstrating the depth of my love and commitment to your well-being.

"I am the resurrection and the life." In this, I offer the promise of eternal life, triumph over death, and the hope of resurrection for all who believe in me. I am the source of true life, both in this world and in the world to come.

"I am the way, the truth, and the life." I am the exclusive path to the Father, the embodiment of truth, and the giver of abundant life. Through me, you can find reconciliation, understanding, and purpose.

"I am the true Vine." I am the root from which spiritual sustenance flows, the source of your nourishment and growth. As you remain connected to me, you will bear fruit and experience the fullness of life in abundance.

When these "I am" statements are considered together, the deeper meaning becomes clear. I am your all in all – the provider of sustenance for your soul, the light that shines in your darkness, the gate to salvation, the loving and protective Shepherd, the conqueror of death, the way to the Father, and the source of spiritual nourishment. I am the completeness of your existence, the fulfillment of your deepest longings, and the embodiment of truth and love.

In declaring these "I am" statements, I want you to understand that my purpose is to reveal the nature of God, to bring you into a loving relationship with Him, and to offer you the opportunity to experience eternal life in all its fullness.

I am the manifestation of God's love, grace, and truth to the world.

Through these "I am" declarations, I want you to know that I have come so that you may have life and have it abundantly. I am the embodiment of complete spiritual fulfillment, and I invite you to abide in me, to trust in me, and to find your true purpose and fulfillment in our union.

May you find peace, hope, and meaning in understanding the depth of my purpose and the completeness of my love for you.

With all my love,
Jesus

The clarity of Jesus

The essence of Jesus can be summarized as the all-encompassing source of spiritual sustenance and guidance, providing access to eternal life, truth, and intimate connection with God.

Jesus seven I am finding myself in the context of Jesus

It's truly beautiful to feel a deep sense of gratitude for the ways in which your understanding of Jesus has shaped your values and actions. Understanding yourself in the context of Jesus can be a transformative and enriching experience that brings depth and purpose to your life.

Gratitude is a powerful emotion that can strengthen your connection to your faith and your understanding of Jesus. Take time to reflect on specific instances where your values and actions have been influenced by your understanding of Jesus. Consider the moments when you have shown love, compassion, forgiveness, and empathy, and recognize the ways in which these behaviors align with the teachings of Jesus.

Acknowledging the impact of Jesus on your life can also lead to a deep sense of purpose and fulfillment. By recognizing the alignment between your values and actions with the teachings of Jesus, you affirm the significance of your faith in shaping your character and guiding your choices.

Furthermore, knowing yourself in the context of Jesus can provide a sense of belonging and connection to something greater than yourself. It allows you to see your life as part of a meaningful and purposeful narrative, rooted in love, grace, and the pursuit of righteousness.

Expressing gratitude for the ways in which your understanding of Jesus has influenced your values and actions can also inspire and uplift others. Your genuine appreciation for the transformative power of faith can serve as a source of encouragement and hope for those around you, fostering a spirit of unity and compassion.

As you continue to explore the depths of your faith and your relationship with Jesus, may the sense of gratitude you feel serve as a guiding light, illuminating the path of self-discovery and spiritual growth. Embrace this gratitude as a source of strength and motivation in your ongoing journey of aligning your values and actions with the teachings of Jesus, and allow it to inspire others to embark on their own paths of faith and self-awareness.

Jesus, the 7 I am exclusive to Jesus ONLY

The "I am" statements attributed to Jesus in the Bible are indeed unique to Him and hold a special significance within Christian theology. These statements are found in the Gospel of John and are traditionally understood to convey specific aspects of Jesus' identity and mission. The "I am" statements are considered a crucial part of the New Testament's portrayal of Jesus and are central to understanding His divinity and purpose.

In the Gospel of John, Jesus makes several "I am" declarations, each of which carries profound theological meaning. For instance, He describes Himself as the "bread of life," the "light of the world," the "door of the sheep," the "good shepherd," the "resurrection and the life," the "way, the truth, and the life," and the "true vine."

These statements are significant because they go beyond mere self-identification and reveal essential truths about Jesus' nature and His role in the salvation of humanity. The "I am" declarations emphasize Jesus' divine attributes, His unique relationship with God, and His redemptive mission as the Savior of the world.

While the "I am" statements are exclusive to Jesus within the context of the New Testament, they are meant to convey His unparalleled significance and the profound impact of His teachings on the Christian faith. They serve as powerful affirmations of Jesus' divine nature and His central role in the reconciliation of humankind with God.

It's important to note that the "I am" statements are viewed as foundational to Christian belief and are not typically associated with other individuals. Rather, they are distinct declarations made by Jesus to articulate His divine identity and the transformative power of His teachings.

In summary, the "I am" statements attributed to Jesus are considered unique and exclusive to Him within the context of Christian theology. They are central to the New Testament's portrayal of Jesus and play a significant role in emphasizing His divine nature, His redemptive mission, and His unparalleled significance within the Christian faith.

Confession unto Jesus

My Beloved Child,

I am writing to you today to share the immeasurable love and compassion that I have for you. I want to reveal to you the power of confessing and believing in your heart that I have done everything for your behalf and the transformation that takes place in your life as a result.

First and foremost, I want you to know how much I love you. My sacrifice on the cross and the victory over death were all for you. I long for you to experience the fullness of life that comes from confessing and believing in me. It brings me immense joy to see you embrace the truth and walk in the freedom and redemption that I have secured for you.

Confessing with your mouth that I am your Lord and believing in your heart that I was raised from the dead empowers you to receive the gift of salvation and eternal life. This act of faith is transformative, for it marks the beginning of a new journey - a journey marked by grace, forgiveness, and the assurance of my presence in your life.

When you confess and believe in me, you experience the confirmation of your salvation. You are no longer bound by guilt, shame, or the weight of your past mistakes. Instead, you are set free by the power of my love and the work of redemption that I accomplished on your behalf. In me, you find hope, purpose, and an unshakeable foundation for your life.

Moreover, the transformation that takes place in your life through confessing and believing in me is profound. Your heart is renewed, and your spirit is awakened to a newfound sense of purpose and identity. You are no longer defined by your past, but rather by the abundant grace and love that I bestow upon you.

As you walk in the light of my truth, you will experience the richness of a life filled with my presence. Your faith will deepen, your character will be shaped by love, and your heart will overflow with compassion for others. You will find strength in moments of weakness, peace in times of turmoil, and joy that surpasses all understanding.

My dear one, the benefits of confessing and believing in me go beyond this earthly life. You have the assurance of eternal life with me - a life free from pain, sorrow, and separation. I long to dwell with you in perfect harmony, where every tear will be wiped away, and every longing of your heart will be fulfilled.

I am always here for you, ready to guide and comfort you. Embrace the transformation and the confirmation that comes from confessing and believing in me. As you do so, you will experience the fullness of my love and the remarkable work that I desire to accomplish in your life.

With unwavering love and compassion,
Jesus

Chapter 3

ରଃ୫

I Can See Clearly Now: The Oneness of Jesus and Man

Divine Encounter: Surrendering to The I Am

Jesus said we are joint heirs with Him

Joint heirs: not of the world

Joint heirs: Reflection of The Light

Joint heirs: Reflection of The Door

Joint heirs: Reflection of The Good Shepherd

Joint heirs: Reflection of The Resurrection and the Life

Joint heirs: Reflection of The Way, The Truth, and The Life

Joint heirs: Reflection of The True Vine

Joint heirs: Reflection of The 7 I Am

Joint heirs: The 7 I am Statements and 1 Corinthians 3:6-9

Chapter 3

(continued)

ॐ

I Can See Clearly Now: The Oneness of Jesus and Man

Living as the Bread of Life

Living as the Light of the World

Living as the Door

Living as the Good Shepherd

Living as the Resurrection and the Life

Living as the Way, the Truth, and the Life

Living as the Vine

We are Ambassador for Christ

The appointment as an "Ambassador for Christ"

The "I am" statements of Jesus from the Bible are significant declarations made by Jesus Himself, affirming His divine nature and identity. Each statement provides insight into different aspects of who Jesus is and His role in the world. Here are the seven "I am" statements of Jesus as recorded in the Gospel of John:

1. "I am the bread of life." (John 6:35) This statement emphasizes Jesus as the source of spiritual nourishment and sustenance for all who believe in Him.

2. "I am the light of the world." (John 8:12) Here, Jesus proclaims himself as the source of truth and guidance, shining light in the darkness of the world.

3. "I am the door of the sheep." (John 10:7) Jesus portrays Himself as the gateway to salvation and eternal life, the only way for people to enter into a relationship with God.

4. "I am the good shepherd." (John 10:11) This statement reveals Jesus' role as the caring and protective shepherd who lays down His life for His sheep, symbolizing His sacrificial love for humanity.

5. "I am the resurrection and the life." (John 11:25) By identifying Himself as the resurrection and the life, Jesus asserts His power over death and offers the promise of eternal life to those who believe in Him.

6. **"I am the way, the truth, and the life."** (John 14:6) In This statement, Jesus declares Himself as the exclusive path to God, the embodiment of truth, and the source of abundant and everlasting life.

7. **"I am the true vine."** (John 15:1) Jesus compares Himself to a vine, illustrating the intimate connection between believers (branches) and Himself (the vine), emphasizing the necessity of abiding in Him to bear fruit and grow spiritually.

These "I am" statements collectively depict Jesus as the unique Son of God, the Savior of the world, and the ultimate source of hope, truth, and eternal life for all who put their faith in Him.

Divine Encounter: Surrendering to the I Am

As for discovering your own identity, it is essential to recognize that every individual possesses unique qualities, experiences, and potential. Your identity is shaped by a combination of factors such as your personality, beliefs, values, talents, interests, and relationships.

One way to explore your identity is through self-reflection. Consider what values and beliefs are important to you, what activities bring you joy and fulfillment, and what strengths and weaknesses you possess. Reflect on your life experiences, challenges you have overcome, and moments of personal growth.

It can also be helpful to seek feedback from others who know you well, as their perspective can provide insights into how you are perceived by others. Engage in activities that align with your interests and passions, as these can help you discover more about yourself and what brings meaning to your life.

Remember that identity is a journey, and it is okay if you are still exploring and evolving in your understanding of who you are. Embrace the process of self-discovery, be open to new experiences, and continue to cultivate a sense of authenticity and purpose in your life.

Drawing inspiration from the seven "I am" statements of Jesus, I can offer you a reflection on potential facets of your identity based on these concepts:

1. Bread of Life. Just as Jesus identified Himself as the bread of life, you might reflect on how you can be a source of nourishment and sustenance to others. Consider how you can offer support, encouragement, and kindness to those around you, providing them with the spiritual and emotional sustenance they need.

2. Light of the World. Reflect on how you can be a beacon of light in the darkness, spreading positivity, hope, and guidance to those in need. Your words and actions have the power to illuminate the lives of others and inspire them to strive for the betterment of themselves and society.

3. Door of the Sheep. Think about how you can be a gateway for others to find their way to new opportunities, personal growth, or spiritual fulfillment. Consider how you can open doors for those who need assistance or support, helping them navigate life's challenges and find their purpose.

4. Good Shepherd. Reflect on how you can embody qualities of care, compassion, and leadership in your relationships and interactions. You have the potential to be a source of comfort and protection to those around you, guiding them with wisdom and love.

5. Resurrection and Life. Consider how you can be a source of renewal and transformation in the lives of others. Reflect on how your actions and words can bring about new beginnings, hope, and a sense of purpose to those who may be struggling or feeling lost.

6. Way, Truth, and Life. Reflect on how you can be a source of guidance, honesty, and vitality in your interactions with others. Strive to embody integrity, authenticity, and a sense of purpose in all that you do, serving as a role model for those around you.

7. True Vine. Consider how you can foster connection, growth, and community in your relationships and spheres of influence. Reflect on how you can nurture and support others, helping them flourish and thrive in their endeavors.

Ultimately, your identity is a multifaceted and evolving journey that is uniquely yours. By reflecting on these aspects inspired by the "I am" statements of Jesus, you can explore and embrace the ways in which you can positively impact the world around you, express your values and beliefs, and grow into the best version of yourself. Embrace your potential to embody qualities of compassion, leadership, renewal, and connection, and strive to make a difference in the lives of those you encounter on your journey.

Jesus said we are joint heirs with Him

The term "joint heirs" in the Bible refers to the belief that as followers of Jesus, we share in His inheritance as children of God. It signifies that we are co-heirs with Christ, partaking in the blessings and promises of God's kingdom. This concept is found in Romans 8:17 (NIV) which states, "Now if we are children, then we are heirs - heirs of God and co-heirs with Christ, if indeed we share in His sufferings in order that we may also share in His glory."

When Jesus proclaimed that He is the bread of life, He was emphasizing that through Him, we find sustenance and eternal life. As joint heirs with Christ, this means that we inherit not only His divine nature but also the promises and blessings of God's kingdom. To reflect this joint heirship with Christ, we must align our lives with His teachings and example. This includes following His commandments, nurturing a deep relationship with God through prayer and scripture, showing love and compassion to others, and striving to live a life that reflects Christ's love, grace, and selflessness. By embodying these qualities and seeking to imitate Christ in our thoughts, words, and actions, we can truly reflect our status as joint heirs with him.

To exemplify yourself as Jesus, the bread of life, you can start by nourishing yourself spiritually with His teachings and embodying His qualities in your daily life. Here are some practical ways to reflect the concept of Jesus as the bread of life:

1. Nourish your spiritual life. Just as bread nourishes the body, seek to feed your soul by diving into the Word of God through reading the Bible regularly, attending church services, engaging in prayer, and participating in spiritual practices that deepen your connection with God.

2. Share the "bread" with others. Just as bread is meant to be shared, look for opportunities to share the love, grace, and message of Jesus with those around you. This could involve acts of kindness, serving others in need, showing compassion and empathy, and being a source of hope and light in the lives of those you encounter.

3. Be a source of sustenance. As the bread of life sustains us, we strive to be a source of encouragement, support, and positivity to those who may be struggling or in need of nourishment. Offer a listening ear, provide comfort, and be a reflection of Christ's love to those who are hungry for hope and healing.

4. Seek to satisfy spiritual hunger. Just as bread can satisfy physical hunger, aim to satisfy spiritual hunger by pointing others towards the source of true fulfillment and purpose - Jesus Christ. Share His message of salvation, redemption, and eternal life with those who are seeking meaning and truth.

5. Live out Christ's teachings. Finally, embody the teachings and example of Jesus in your everyday life. Seek to be a reflection of His love, compassion, forgiveness, and humility in all that you do. By walking in His footsteps and allowing His light to shine through you, you can exemplify yourself as Jesus, the bread of life, to the world around you.

By incorporating these practices into your life and striving to reflect the essence of Jesus as the bread of life, you can inspire others and draw closer to God as you live out your faith in a tangible and impactful way.

Joint heirs: not of the world

When Jesus spoke about being "not of the world" as He was with the Father, He was highlighting the idea that as followers of Christ, our values, priorities, and way of life are distinct from the worldly norms and standards. As joint heirs with Christ, this concept calls us to live in the world but not be conformed to its ways, to be set apart in our beliefs and actions, reflecting our identity as children of God. Here's how this concept applies to us and how we can become a reflection of being joint heirs with Christ:

1. Separation from worldly values. To be "not of the world" means aligning our values with the teachings of Christ rather than conforming to the materialism, selfishness, and immorality that often dominate worldly attitudes. This involves prioritizing spiritual growth, integrity, humility, and love over worldly success, greed, and self-centeredness.

2. Living out our identity. As joint heirs with Christ, we are called to live out our identity as children of God. This means embodying the character of Christ in our attitudes, words, and actions, reflecting His love, grace, and compassion to those around us.

3. Engaging with the world. While we are not of the world, we are still called to engage with it in a way that brings light and hope. This involves being salt and light in the world, sharing the message of Christ through our interactions, serving others in love, and being a positive influence in our communities.

4. Renewing our minds. To be a reflection of being joint heirs with Christ, we need to renew our minds daily through prayer, meditation on scripture, and seeking the guidance of the Holy Spirit. By allowing God to transform our thoughts and attitudes, we can better reflect the values and character of Christ in our lives.

5. Walking in obedience. Ultimately, being a reflection of being joint heirs with Christ involves walking in obedience to His commandments and following His example. This includes loving God with all our heart, soul, and mind, and loving our neighbors as ourselves.

Joint heirs: Reflection of The Light

By embracing our identity as joint heirs with Christ, we are called to live differently than the world around us, demonstrating the transformative power of the Gospel through our lives. Through intentional living, prayerful dependence on God, and a commitment to following Christ wholeheartedly, we can become true reflections of our status as joint heirs with Him, bringing glory to God and drawing others closer to the truth of the Gospel.

To exemplify yourself as a light in the world, following the example of Jesus, you can incorporate the following practices into your life:

1. Live out the teachings of Jesus. Study the life and teachings of Jesus in the Bible and strive to embody His values of love, compassion, humility, and forgiveness in your daily interactions with others.

2. Serve others selflessly. Follow Jesus' example of serving others selflessly by looking for ways to help those in need, show kindness, and extend a helping hand to those around you.

3. Practice empathy and compassion. Show empathy and compassion towards others, just as Jesus did during His ministry on earth. Listen to others with an open heart, seek to understand their perspectives, and offer support and encouragement where needed.

4. Be a peacemaker. Strive to promote peace and reconciliation in your relationships and communities, following Jesus' call to be peacemakers and to seek unity among believers.

5. Share the Gospel. Be willing to share the message of God's love and salvation through Jesus Christ with those around you, whether through your words, actions, or lifestyle. Let your light shine brightly as you share the hope and joy found in Christ.

6. Practice forgiveness. Just as Jesus modeled forgiveness on the cross, strive to forgive those who have wronged you and release any bitterness or resentment in your heart. By extending forgiveness, you reflect the grace and mercy of God to others.

7. Be a voice for justice. Standing up for what is right and speaking out against injustice, oppression, and discrimination, and advocating for the marginalized and vulnerable in society.

8. Pray without ceasing. Maintain a close relationship with God through prayer, seeking His guidance, strength, and wisdom in all areas of your life. Allow the Holy Spirit to work in and through you to be a light in the world.

9. Lead by example. Let your actions speak louder than your words by consistently living out your faith in a way that reflects the character of Christ. Be a role model for others to emulate as they see Christ's light shining through you.

10. Remain rooted in God's word. Stay grounded in the truth of God's word, allowing it to shape your beliefs, values, and worldview. Let the Bible be your guide in all that you do, reflecting the light of Christ in your thoughts, words, and deeds.

By embodying these principles and following the example of Jesus as the light of the world, you can inspire and influence those around you to see the transformative power of God's love and grace. Remember that being a light in the world is not about perfection but about a willingness to show God's love and truth in all that you do, pointing others towards the source of all light and hope - Jesus Christ.

When Jesus declared Himself as the light of the world, He was expressing His role as the source of truth, guidance, and salvation for all humanity. As followers of Christ, we are called to reflect His light in the world and become joint heirs with Him through our relationship with God. Here's how we can apply this concept and become reflection of being joint heirs with Christ:

1. Identity in Christ. Understanding our identity as children of God and joint heirs with Christ is essential. By accepting Christ as our Lord and Savior, we become part of God's family, sharing in the inheritance and blessings that come through our relationship with Him.

2. Reflecting Christ's Character. Just as a mirror reflects light, our lives should reflect the character of Christ. This means living in accordance with His teachings, embodying traits such as love, compassion, humility, grace, and forgiveness.

3. Walking in the Light. Walking in the light means living a life that is aligned with God's truth and righteousness. By seeking to live a life of integrity, honesty, and honor, we reflect the light of Christ and draw others closer to Him.

4. Sharing the Gospel. As joint heirs with Christ, we are called to share the good news of salvation with others. By proclaiming the message of God's love, grace, and redemption, we become instruments of His light in a world that desperately needs hope.

5. Serving Others. Following Christ's example of servanthood, we are called to serve others with love and humility. By reaching out to those in need, showing kindness, and meeting practical needs, we demonstrate the light of Christ in action.

6. Living in Unity. As joint heirs with Christ, we are part of a larger body of believers who make up the church. By cultivating unity, fellowship, and mutual support within the body of Christ, we reflect the unity and love that exists within the Godhead.

7. Prayer and Dependence on God. Maintaining a close relationship with God through prayer, worship, and studying of His Word is essential for reflecting Christ's light. By depending on God's strength, wisdom, and guidance, we demonstrate our reliance on Him as our source of light and life.

8. Growing in Faith. Growing in our faith and trust in God is key to becoming effective reflections of Christ's light. By deepening our understanding of God's love and promises, we can face challenges with courage and hope, pointing others to the source of our faith.

9. Perseverance and Endurance. Just as Christ endured hardships and suffering for the sake of humanity, we are called to persevere in our faith journey. By facing trials with faith, patience, and resilience, we demonstrate our commitment to following Christ and shining His light in the world.

10. Hope in Christ's Return. As joint heirs with Christ, we place our ultimate hope in His return and the fulfillment of God's kingdom. By living in anticipation of Christ's second coming, we reflect the light of hope and assurance that comes from our future inheritance in Him.

By applying these principles and seeking to reflect the light of Christ in all that we do, we can become effective witnesses of God's love, grace, and truth in a world that is in desperate need of His light. As joint heirs with Christ, we have the privilege and responsibility of shining His light brightly in the darkness, pointing others to the source of all light and life - Jesus Christ.

Exemplifying yourself as the light of the world, following the example of Christ, involves embodying qualities and behaviors that reflect His character and teachings. Here are some ways you can exemplify yourself as Christ's light:

1. Love and Compassion. Show love and compassion to all people, regardless of their background or beliefs. Treat others with kindness, empathy, and understanding, just as Jesus did during His time on earth.

2. Forgiveness. Practice forgiveness towards those who have wronged you, just as Christ forgave us. Let go of resentment, anger, and strive to reconcile and restore relationships whenever possible.

3. Humility. Humble yourself by putting others' needs before your own and serving them with a genuine heart. Avoid pride and selfishness and seek to emulate Christ's humility in your interactions with others.

4. Truth and Integrity. Be a beacon of truth and integrity in all your words and actions. Honor your commitments, speak honestly, and stand up for what is right, even when it is difficult.

5. Generosity. Share your time, resources, and talents generously with those in need. Show kindness through acts of giving, whether through charity work, donations, or simply helping those around you.

6. Faithfulness. Remain steadfast in your faith and trust in God, even in the face of challenges and uncertainties. Reflect Christ's unwavering faithfulness by staying committed to your beliefs and values.

7. Prayer and Spiritual Growth. Cultivate a strong prayer life and seek spiritual growth through studying the Bible and participating in a Christian community. Draw strength and wisdom from God through prayer and reflection on His Word.

8. Encouragement and Support. Lift others up with words of encouragement, support, and affirmation. Be a source of hope and inspiration to those around you, offering a listening ear and a helping hand when needed.

9. Peace and Reconciliation. Strive to be a peacemaker in conflicts and seek reconciliation in broken relationships. Work towards unity and understanding, promoting harmony and cooperation among all people.

10. Joy and Gratitude. Let your life be characterized by joy and gratitude, regardless of your circumstances. Express thankfulness for the blessings in your life and spread joy to others through your positive attitude and outlook.

By embodying these qualities and behaviors inspired by the teachings of Christ, you can exemplify yourself as the light of the world. Remember that as you strive to reflect Christ's light, you are not alone; God's grace and strength are always available to guide and empower you on your journey. Let your light shine brightly for others to see, pointing them towards the love, grace, and truth of Jesus Christ.

Joint heirs: Reflection of The Door

When Jesus referred to Himself as the door and mentioned believers as joint heirs with Him, He was illustrating the intimate relationship and shared inheritance that Christians have with Him. As joint heirs with Christ, believers are granted a special position of privilege and responsibility, sharing in the blessings and promises of God's kingdom. Here's how this concept applies to us and how we can reflect our status as joint heirs with Christ:

1. Identity in Christ. As joint heirs with Christ, our identity is rooted in Him. We are adopted into God's family, co-heirs with Jesus, and recipients of His grace and salvation. This identity shapes how we view ourselves and others, knowing that we are loved, valued, and cherished by God.

2. Inheritance of Blessings. As joint heirs with Christ, we inherit the spiritual blessings and promises of God's kingdom. This includes forgiveness of sins, eternal life, and access to God's presence, and the empowerment of the Holy Spirit. We are called to live with gratitude and humility, recognizing the abundance of God's grace in our lives.

3. Relationship with God. Being joint heirs with Christ means we have a close relationship with God the Father. Through Jesus, we have access to the Father's love, guidance, and provision. We are invited to communicate with

God through prayer, seeking His will and trusting in His faithfulness.

4. Servanthood and Mission. Reflecting our status as joint heirs with Christ involves living out His example of servanthood and mission. Just as Jesus came not to be served but to serve, we are called to serve others in love, compassion, and humility. This includes sharing the message of salvation and making disciples of all nations.

5. Suffering and Glory. As joint heirs with Christ, we may also share in His suffering and persecution. Jesus endured hardship and rejection for the sake of the gospel, and we too, may face challenges for our faith. Yet, we can take comfort in the promise of sharing in Christ's glory and resurrection.

6. Holiness and Transformation. Reflecting our identity as joint heirs with Christ involves pursuing holiness and living a life transformed by His grace. We are called to grow in faith, wisdom, and maturity, allowing the Holy Spirit to work in us and conform us to the image of Christ.

7. Community and Unity. As joint heirs with Christ, we are part of the body of believers, united in fellowship and purpose. We are called to build up one another in love, support each other in times of need, and demonstrate unity in diversity as followers of Christ.

To become a reflection of being joint heirs with Christ, we must continually seek to align our lives with the teachings and example of Jesus. This process involves cultivating a deep relationship with God, growing in faith and obedience, and living out the values of the kingdom of God in our daily interactions with others.

By surrendering our will to God, seeking His guidance through prayer and scripture, and allowing the Holy Spirit to transform us from the inside out, we can increasingly reflect the light and love of Christ to the world. Remember that being joint heirs with Christ is a privilege and a calling that requires humility, faithfulness, and a willingness to follow His lead in all areas of our lives.

To exemplify yourself as Christ being the door means reflecting the qualities and teachings of Jesus as the doorway to God's kingdom and salvation. Here are some ways you can embody the concept of Christ as the door in your life:

1. Welcoming and Inclusive. Just as a door provides access to a space, strive to be welcoming and inclusive to all people. Show love, kindness, and acceptance to those around you, regardless of their background, beliefs, or circumstances.

2. Gateway to Hope. Be a source of hope and encouragement to others, pointing them towards the ultimate hope found in Christ. Share the message of salvation and eternal life that Jesus offers as the door to God's kingdom.

3. Protection and Security. Serve as a protector and supporter for those in need, offering a sense of security and stability in a tumultuous world. Stand up for justice, defend the vulnerable, and provide a safe haven for those seeking refuge.

4. Bridge Builder. Act as a bridge between people and God, helping others connect with the divine presence and experience spiritual growth. Share your faith journey, offer guidance and support, and model a life surrendered to God.

5. Gatekeeper of Truth. Uphold the truth of God's word and the teachings of Jesus, serving as a gatekeeper against falsehood and deception. Seek wisdom and discernment to navigate the complexities of life and guide others towards righteousness.

6. Servant Leadership. Embrace the servant leadership exemplified by Jesus, humbly serving others and putting their needs above your own. Lead by example, demonstrating selflessness, compassion, and integrity in all you do.

7. Invitation to Transformation. Encourage personal growth and transformation in yourself and others, inviting them to step through the door of change and renewal offered by Christ. Support spiritual development, offer resources for growth, and provide a listening ear for those seeking guidance.

8. Bridge of Communication. Foster open and honest communication with others, creating a bridge for dialogue, understanding, and reconciliation. Help bridge divides, heal broken relationships, and facilitate unity in diversity.

9. Provider of Comfort. Offer comfort, solace, and encouragement to those who are struggling or in pain, demonstrating the compassion and empathy of Christ. Walk alongside others in their challenges, offering a listening ear and a caring heart.

10. Bearer of Light. Shine the light of Christ in a dark world, illuminating the path to truth, righteousness, and salvation. Be a beacon of hope, joy, and love, reflecting the glory of God in everything you do.

By embodying these qualities and actions in your life, you can exemplify yourself as Christ being the door; a gateway to God's kingdom, a source of hope and salvation, and a reflection of His love and grace to those around you.

Remember that it is through your words and deeds that you can demonstrate the transformative power of Christ as the door, inviting others to experience His abundant life and eternal blessings.

Joint heirs: Reflection of The Good Shepherd

When Jesus referred to Himself as the Good Shepherd, He highlighted His role in caring for and guiding His followers, just as a shepherd tends to His sheep. As joint heirs with Christ, we are called to reflect His qualities and fulfill our role as co-heirs of God's kingdom. Here's how this concept applies to us and how we can become a reflection of being joint heirs with Christ:

1. Shepherding Others. Just as Jesus shepherds His flock with love, compassion, and wisdom, we are called to shepherd and care for those around us. This means leading by example, offering guidance and support, and nurturing spiritual growth in others.

2. Sacrificial Love. The Good Shepherd lays down His life for His sheep out of love. As joint heirs with Christ, we are called to embody sacrificial love in our relationships, willing to make sacrifices for the well-being of others and to demonstrate Christ-like love in all that we do.

3. Protection and Provision. The Good Shepherd protects His flock from harm and provides for their needs. As joint heirs with Christ, we are called to protect and support those in need, offering a safe and nurturing environment for growth and flourishing.

4. Unity and Community. The shepherd brings together His flock, fostering unity and community among the sheep. As joint heirs with Christ, we are called to promote unity in the body of Christ, building strong and supportive communities where love, respect, and collaboration flourish.

5. Guidance and Direction. The shepherd leads His sheep to green pastures and still waters, guiding them along the right path. As joint heirs with Christ, we are called to provide guidance and direction to others, helping them navigate life's challenges and make choices that align with God's will.

6. Faithfulness and Commitment. The Good Shepherd is faithful and committed to His flock, never abandoning them. As joint heirs with Christ, we are called to demonstrate faithfulness and commitment in our relationships, remaining steadfast in our love and support for others.

7. Forgiveness and Reconciliation. The Good Shepherd offers forgiveness and reconciliation to His sheep, restoring broken relationships and healing wounds. As joint heirs with Christ, we are called to practice forgiveness and seek reconciliation, extending grace and compassion to those who have wronged us.

8. Servant Leadership. The shepherd serves His flock with humility and selflessness, putting their needs above His own. As joint heirs with Christ, we are called to embrace servant leadership, serving others with humility, compassion, and integrity.

9. Empowerment and Empathy. The Good Shepherd empowers His sheep, giving them courage and strength to face challenges. As joint heirs with Christ, we are called to empower others, offering them support, encouragement, and empathy in their journey of faith and growth.

10. Eternal Inheritance. As joint heirs with Christ, we share in the inheritance of God's kingdom and the promise of eternal life. By living out our faith, reflecting Christ's love and grace, and embodying the qualities of the Good Shepherd, we bear witness to our status as co-heirs with Christ and invite others to join us in experiencing the abundant blessings of God's kingdom.

By embracing these principles and striving to embody the characteristics of the Good Shepherd in our own lives, we can become a reflection of being joint heirs with Christ, sharing in His mission of love, service, and redemption for the world. Let us seek to emulate Christ's example of shepherding, love, and sacrifice, as we walk together as co-heirs of the kingdom of God.

To exemplify Christ as the Good Shepherd in your own life, you can strive to embody His qualities and characteristics through your actions, attitudes, and relationships. Here are some practical ways to reflect the attributes of the Good Shepherd in your daily life:

1. Caring for Others. Show genuine care and compassion for those around you, just as the Good Shepherd cares for His sheep. Take the time to listen, offer a helping hand, and be present for others in their times of need.

2. Leading by Example. Lead with integrity and humility, setting a positive example for others to follow. Just as the Good Shepherd leads His flock, you can lead by serving, inspiring, and guiding others toward goodness and truth.

3. Sacrificial Love. Practice sacrificial love by putting the needs of others above your own desires. Show kindness, forgiveness, and grace, even when it is difficult or inconvenient.

4. Protecting and Providing. Look out for the well-being of those in your care, providing support and protection as needed. Offer a safe and nurturing environment where others can grow and thrive.

5. Building Community. Foster unity and community among your relationships and within your community. Encourage cooperation, respect, and understanding among diverse groups of people.

6. Offering Guidance. Provide wisdom and guidance to others, helping them navigate life's challenges and make choices aligned with God's will. Be a source of encouragement and support for those who look to you for advice.

7. Remaining Faithful. Stay true to your commitments and relationships, displaying unwavering faithfulness and loyalty like the Good Shepherd. Show up for others in both good times and bad, demonstrating your reliability and trustworthiness.

8. Seeking Reconciliation. Practice forgiveness, reconciliation, and peacemaking in your relationships. Be willing to extend grace and seek unity, even in times of conflict or disagreement.

9. Serving with Humility. Serve others with humility and selflessness, putting their needs before your own. Look for opportunities to serve those who are less fortunate or in need of assistance.

10. Empowering Others. Encourage and empower others to reach their full potential. Offer support, guidance, and resources to help others grow and succeed in their own journeys.

By actively embodying these traits and qualities in your daily life, you can exemplify Christ as the Good Shepherd and reflect His love, compassion, and grace to those around you. Remember that it is through the power of the Holy Spirit and your willingness to follow Christ's example that you can truly shine as a beacon of His light in the world. Let your actions speak louder than words and allow Christ to work through you to shepherd and care for those in your midst.

Joint heirs: Reflection of The Resurrection and the Life

When Jesus declared that He is the resurrection and the life, He was proclaiming His role as the source of eternal life and the power to overcome death. As joint heirs with Christ, believers are invited to share in His inheritance and experience the fullness of His resurrection power in their lives. Here's how this applies to us and how we can become reflections of being joint heirs with Christ:

1. Embracing Salvation. As joint heirs with Christ, we have been adopted into God's family through faith in Jesus Christ. By accepting His sacrifice on the cross for our sins and receiving the gift of salvation, we become heirs to the promise of eternal life and reconciliation with God.

2. Living in Victory. Through Christ's resurrection, we have the assurance of victory over sin, death, and all the powers of darkness. As joint heirs, we can walk in confidence, knowing that we are empowered by the same Spirit that raised Jesus from the dead.

3. Identifying with Christ. To reflect our identity as joint heirs with Christ, we must strive to align our thoughts, actions, and beliefs with His teachings and example. This includes living a life of obedience to God's word, walking in love and humility, and seeking to imitate Christ's character in all that we do.

4. Participating in His Mission. As joint heirs with Christ, we are called to partner with Him in His mission to bring restoration, healing, and hope to a broken world. By sharing the good news of the gospel, serving others in love, and living out our faith authentically, we bear witness to our identity as heirs of God's kingdom.

5. Seeking Unity with Christ. Cultivating a deep and intimate relationship with Christ is essential to reflecting our identity as joint heirs. Through prayer, worship, studying God's word, and participating in fellowship with other believers, we can draw closer to Him and experience the richness of our inheritance in Him.

6. Walking in Faith. Trusting in God's promises and exercising faith in His provision is key to manifesting our identity as joint heirs with Christ. By stepping out in faith, even when circumstances seem challenging or uncertain, we demonstrate our confidence in God's faithfulness and power to fulfill His purposes in our lives.

7. Serving Others. Reflecting Christ as joint heirs also involves serving others with compassion, grace, and selflessness. Just as Jesus came to serve and not to be served, we are called to follow His example by caring for the needs of those around us and extending love to all people.

8. Embracing the Hope of Glory. As joint heirs with Christ, we have the hope of sharing in His glory and eternal kingdom. By fixing our eyes on this ultimate reality and living with an eternal perspective, we can withstand trials, overcome challenges, and remain steadfast in our faith.

To become reflections of being joint heirs with Christ, we must daily surrender our lives to Him, allowing His Holy Spirit to transform us from the inside out. By abiding in Christ, seeking to walk in His footsteps, and trusting in His unfailing love and grace, we can bear witness to the world of our shared inheritance as beloved children of God.

To exemplify yourself as Jesus, the resurrection, and the life, you can incorporate the following principles into your life:

1. Faith in His Power. Just as Jesus is the resurrection and the life, trust in His power to bring new life and transformation to every situation. Approach challenges with faith, knowing that through Christ, there is always hope and a way forward.

2. Living with Purpose. Like Jesus, live with a sense of purpose and mission. Seek to bring life, hope, and healing to those around you by sharing the message of the gospel and demonstrating love in action.

3. Prioritizing Relationship. Jesus valued relationships and spent time with people, showing them love and compassion. Take the time to build authentic connections with others, listen with empathy, and offer support and encouragement.

4. Embracing Resurrection Living. Allow the power of Christ's resurrection to shape your daily life. Walk in the freedom and victory that comes from knowing that you are a new creation in Christ, released from the power of sin and death.

5. Extending Grace. Just as Jesus offers forgiveness and grace to all, seek to extend the same grace to those around you. Practice forgiveness, show compassion, and treat others with kindness, reflecting the love of Christ in your interactions.

6. Sharing Hope. Be a source of hope and encouragement to others, pointing them towards the ultimate hope found in Jesus. Share your faith boldly and testify to the ways in which Christ has brought new life and purpose to your own story.

7. Being a Light in Darkness. In a world filled with brokenness and despair, be a light that shines brightly by reflecting the hope and love of Jesus. Offer a listening ear, a helping hand, and a message of comfort to those who are struggling.

8. Living in Resurrection Power. Allow the Holy Spirit to work in and through you, transforming your life and empowering you to live as a witness to Christ's resurrection power. Walk in obedience to God's word and be open to the leading of the Spirit in all areas of your life.

9. Seeking Unity with Christ. Cultivate a deep and intimate relationship with Jesus through prayer, worship, and studying the Scriptures. Allow His presence to permeate every aspect of your life, guiding your decisions and shaping your character.

10. Walking in Love. Above all, strive to embody the love of Christ in all that you do. Love sacrificially, forgive freely, and serve selflessly, demonstrating the unconditional love that Jesus has shown to you.

By incorporating these principles into your daily life and seeking to exemplify Jesus as the resurrection and the life, you can become a beacon of hope, a source of life, and a reflection of Christ's love to those around you. Remember that it is through abiding in Him and allowing His Spirit to work in and through you that you can truly reflect His transformative power and life-giving presence to the world.

Joint heirs:
Reflection of The Way, The Truth, and The Life

When Jesus declared that He is the way, the truth, and the life, He was describing the foundational role He plays in leading humanity to the Father, revealing divine truth, and offering eternal life. As joint heirs with Christ, we are called to embody these qualities and reflect His character to the world.

To become a reflection of being joint heirs with Christ, consider the following steps:

1. Understanding Our Identity in Christ. Recognize that as believers, we are adopted into God's family and share in the inheritance of Christ. This means we have access to the same privileges, blessings, and authority that Jesus has as the Son of God.

2. Walking in the Way. Emulate Jesus as the way by following His teachings, living a life marked by obedience to God's word, and walking in alignment with His will. Strive to imitate His example of humility, service, and love towards others.

3. Embracing the Truth. Seek to align your beliefs, values, and actions with the truth of God's Word. Allow the Holy Spirit to guide you into all truth, deepen your understanding of God's plans and purposes, and live a life grounded in the unchanging truths of Scripture.

4. Embodying the Life. Reflect the life of Christ by bearing fruits of the Spirit, such as love, joy, peace, patience, kindness, goodness, faithfulness, gentleness, and self-control. Allow the life of Christ to flow through you, bringing transformation and renewal to your inner being and outward expressions.

5. Living as Joint Heirs. Recognize your co-heir status with Christ, which signifies your inheritance of salvation, eternal life, and the promises of God's kingdom. Live in the fullness of this inheritance, knowing that you are a child of God and a co-heir with Christ.

6. Serving Others. Just as Jesus came not to be served but to serve, seek opportunities to serve and bless others selflessly. Use your gifts, talents, and resources to impact the lives of those around you, reflecting the heart of Christ in your acts of service and compassion.

7. Seeking Unity with Christ. Cultivate a deep and intimate relationship with Jesus through prayer, worship, and fellowship. Abide in Him daily, allowing His presence to transform your heart and shape your character to reflect His own.

8. Walking in Faith. Trust in the promises of God and walk by faith, knowing that as joint heirs with Christ, you are called to live a life of faithfulness, courage, and perseverance. Trust in God's provision, guidance, and sovereignty in all circumstances.

9. Sharing the Good News. As joint heirs with Christ, you are called to be ambassadors of His kingdom, sharing the message of salvation and reconciliation with others. Proclaim the good news of Jesus Christ with boldness, compassion, and love, inviting others to experience the life-transforming power of the gospel.

10. Abiding in Love. Above all, let love be the hallmark of your life as a joint heir with Christ. Love God with all your heart, soul, mind, and strength, and love your neighbor as yourself. Let the love of Christ flow through you, drawing others to the source of all love and life.

By embodying these qualities and principles, you can reflect the reality of being joint heirs with Christ to the world. Live in the fullness of your identity in Christ, walking in His way, embodying His truth, and reflecting His life to those around you. Let your life be a testament to the transformative power of being united with Christ as joint heirs in God's kingdom.

To exemplify yourself as Jesus being the way, the truth, and the life, you can incorporate the following principles into your daily life:

1. Embrace Jesus as the Way. Follow Jesus' teachings and example in all aspects of your life. Prioritize your relationship with God and seek His will in all that you do. Live with integrity, honesty, and humility, reflecting the character of Jesus in your actions and decisions.

2. Embody Jesus as the Truth. Ground your beliefs and values in the truth of God's Word. Speak the truth in love, being a person of honesty and integrity. Seek wisdom and understanding through prayer, study of Scripture, and guidance from the Holy Spirit.

3. Reflect Jesus as the Life. Cultivate a vibrant and authentic relationship with God through prayer, worship, and fellowship. Live a life marked by love, joy, peace, and compassion, reflecting the abundant life that Jesus offers. Share the hope and eternal life found in Christ with others through your words and actions.

4. Walk in the Way of Love. Love unconditionally and sacrificially, following Jesus' command to love God and love your neighbor as yourself. Show kindness, compassion, and empathy to those around you, demonstrating the love of Christ in practical ways. Forgive others as Christ has forgiven you, extending grace and reconciliation in your relationships.

5. Speak the Truth in Love. Communicate with honesty, gentleness, and respect, avoiding falsehood and deceit. Stand firm in your beliefs and convictions, while also being open to dialogue and understanding differing perspectives. Share the truth of the gospel with grace and compassion, pointing others to the source of ultimate truth found in Jesus.

6. Live a Life of Abundance. Embrace the fullness of life in Christ, experiencing joy, peace, and fulfillment in His presence. Seek to bring life-giving words and actions into your relationships and interactions, uplifting and encouraging others. Share the hope and purpose that comes from a life surrendered to Jesus, inviting others to experience true life in Him.

7. Model Servant Leadership. Serve others selflessly, following Jesus' example of humility and servant leadership. Use your gifts, talents, and resources to bless and empower those in need, reflecting the love and compassion of Christ. Lead by serving; inspiring others to follow the path of Jesus as the ultimate servant-leader.

8. Walk in Faith and Obedience. Trust in God's faithfulness and promises, knowing that He is the way-maker and sustainer of life. Obey God's commands and guidance, surrendering your will to His and walking in faithfulness and obedience. Step out in faith, trusting that Jesus is the way, the truth, and the life, guiding you on the path to abundant living.

By embodying these principles and qualities in your daily life, you can exemplify yourself as Jesus being the way, the truth, and the life to those around you. Let your words and actions reflect the love, truth, and abundant life that Jesus offers, pointing others to the transformative power of His presence and teachings. Strive to be a living example of Christ's character and message, bringing hope, light, and love into the world through your life lived in alignment with His example.

Joint heirs: Reflection of The True Vine

When Jesus said He was the true vine and that we are joint heirs with Him, He was illustrating the intimate and vital connection believers have with Him and the blessings that come from being part of His family. As joint heirs with Christ, we share in His inheritance, His mission, and His relationship with the Father. Here's how this applies to us and how we can reflect being joint heirs with Christ:

1. Abiding in Christ as the True Vine. Just as branches draw nourishment and life from the vine, we are called to abide in Christ, staying connected to him through prayer, worship, and obedience. By maintaining a close relationship with Jesus, we receive spiritual nourishment, guidance, and strength to bear fruit in our lives.

2. Sharing in Christ's Inheritance. As joint heirs with Christ, we inherit the blessings and promises of salvation, eternal life, and a restored relationship with God. Through our union with Christ, we have access to the riches of God's grace, mercy, and love, experiencing the fullness of life that comes from being part of His family.

3. Unity and Communion with Christ. Being joint heirs with Christ emphasizes our unity with Him and with our fellow believers, forming a community of faith that reflects the love and unity of the Trinity. As members of Christ's body, we are called to love one another, support each other, and work together to advance God's kingdom and glorify Him in all that we do.

4. Walking in the Spirit. The Holy Spirit dwells in us as believers, empowering us to live out our identity as joint heirs with Christ and to bear fruit that reflects His character. By yielding to the Spirit's guidance and allowing him to work in and through us, we can demonstrate the love, joy, peace, patience, kindness, goodness, faithfulness, gentleness, and self-control that are the fruit of the Spirit.

5. Serving and Following Christ's Example. As joint heirs with Christ, we are called to follow His example of humility, selflessness, love, and service to others. By imitating Christ's sacrificial love and servant-hearted leadership, we can reflect His character and values to the world, showing compassion and care for those in need.

6. Living in Alignment with God's Will. As joint heirs with Christ, we are called to align our will with God's will, seeking to advance His kingdom and bring glory to His name in all that we do. By praying, studying God's Word, and listening to the leading of the Holy Spirit, we can discern God's purposes for our lives and walk in obedience to His commands.

7. Embracing Our Identity in Christ. Being joint heirs with Christ means that we are beloved children of God, chosen and cherished by Him for a purpose. By affirming our identity in Christ, we can walk in confidence, knowing that we are deeply loved, forgiven, and empowered to live out our faith in a way that honors God and reflects His kingdom values.

8. Sharing the Good News of Salvation. As joint heirs with Christ, we are entrusted with the message of salvation and the hope of eternal life that comes through faith in Jesus. By sharing the good news of the gospel with others and inviting them into relationship with Christ, we participate in God's redemptive work and fulfill our mission as ambassadors of Christ.

In summary, being joint heirs with Christ is a profound and transformative reality that shapes our identity, purpose, and relationships as followers of Jesus. By abiding in Christ, sharing in His inheritance, walking in the Spirit, serving others, aligning with God's will, embracing our identity, and sharing the gospel, we can reflect the love, grace, and power of being united with Christ as His beloved children and co-heirs of God's kingdom.

Exemplifying yourself as Jesus, the true vine, involves cultivating a deep and intimate relationship with Him, bearing fruit that reflects His character and values, and abiding in His love and truth. Here are some practical ways to exemplify yourself as Jesus, the true Vine:

1. Abide in Christ. Prioritize spending time in prayer, reading the Bible, and seeking God's presence to strengthen your relationship with Jesus. Stay connected to the true Vine by maintaining a consistent and vibrant spiritual life that centers on Christ.

2. Bear Fruit. Reflect the fruit of the Spirit in your life by demonstrating love, joy, peace, patience, kindness, goodness, faithfulness, gentleness, and self-control. Use your talents, gifts, and resources to serve others and make a positive impact in your community, reflecting Jesus' compassion and generosity.

3. Stay Connected to the Body of Christ. Engage with a local church or Christian community to grow in fellowship, accountability, and mutual support with other believers. Participate in worship, prayer, and service opportunities that help you stay connected to the larger body of Christ.

4. Follow Jesus' Example. Emulate Jesus' humility, compassion, and selflessness in your interactions with others, seeking to serve and uplift those around you. Practice forgiveness, grace, and reconciliation in your relationships, mirroring Jesus' example of love and reconciliation.

5. Spend Time in Nature. Reflect on the imagery of the vine and branches by spending time in nature and observing how branches draw nourishment and life from the vine. Let the beauty and simplicity of nature remind you of your connection to the true Vine and the importance of abiding in Christ for spiritual growth.

6. Practice Gratitude. Cultivate a spirit of gratitude and thanksgiving for the blessings and provisions in your life, recognizing that all good gifts come from the true Vine. Thank Jesus for His sacrificial love, grace, and redemption, and express your gratitude through prayer, worship, and acts of kindness towards others.

7. Seek Wisdom and Guidance. Seek wisdom and guidance from the Holy Spirit as you navigate life's challenges, decisions, and opportunities, trusting in Jesus as the source of all wisdom and truth. Surrender your will to God's will and seek discernment through prayer, meditation on Scripture, and seeking counsel from wise and trusted mentors.

8. Bear Witness to Jesus. Share your faith and testimony with others by proclaiming the good news of Jesus' love, grace, and salvation to those around you. Live out your faith authentically and courageously, bearing witness to the transforming power of the true Vine in your life and inviting others to experience the life-changing relationship with Jesus.

By exemplifying yourself as Jesus, the true Vine, you can draw strength, nourishment, and purpose from your connection to Him and bear fruit that glorifies God and blesses others. Stay rooted in Christ, abide in His love, and allow His life to flow through you, transforming you into a reflection of His grace, truth, and love in the world.

Joint heirs: Reflection of The 7 I Am

One way to show how you are connected to Jesus as the Bread of Life is by recognizing that He provides spiritual nourishment and sustenance for your soul. Just as bread sustains physical life, Jesus sustains spiritual life through His teachings, presence, and sacrifice. Here's a Bible verse that illustrates this connection:

John 6:35 (NIV). "Then Jesus declared, 'I am the bread of life. Whoever comes to me will never go hungry, and whoever believes in me will never be thirsty.'"

In this verse, Jesus identifies himself as the Bread of Life, emphasizing that those who come to Him will find true satisfaction and fulfillment for their deepest spiritual needs. By applying this verse to your life, you can recognize that your soul finds true nourishment and sustenance in Jesus, just as bread sustains the body.

1. Daily Feeding on the Word of God. Just as bread is a staple food for physical sustenance, make reading and meditating on the Word of God a daily practice for your spiritual nourishment. Spend time in prayer, Bible study, and reflection on the teachings of Jesus to feed your soul and draw closer to him as the Bread of Life.

2. Joining in Fellowship with Believers. Share communion with other believers as a reminder of Jesus' sacrifice and the spiritual nourishment he provides through His body and blood. Participate in worship services, small groups, or Christian gatherings to experience the unity and community of believers who are sustained by Jesus as the Bread of Life.

3. Serving Others with Christ's Love. Use your gifts, resources, and time to serve others in need, following Jesus' example of compassion, generosity, and selflessness. Recognize that by feeding the hungry, caring for the sick, and comforting the broken-hearted, you are embodying the nourishing presence of Jesus as the Bread of Life in the world.

By applying John 6:35 to your life and reflecting on the significance of Jesus as the Bread of Life, you can deepen your understanding of your spiritual hunger and the fulfillment that comes from abiding in Christ. Just as bread sustains physical life, Jesus sustains spiritual life and offers true nourishment and satisfaction for your soul. Seek to abide in Him daily, feed on His Word, and share His love and grace with others as you walk in the truth that Jesus is the Bread of Life for all who come to Him in faith and believe in His name.

As you seek to emulate the concept of being the Bread of Life in your own life, consider these two Bible verses that highlight qualities and actions that can help you reflect the nourishing and life-giving nature of Jesus:

Matthew 5:13-16 (NIV). "You are the salt of the earth. But if the salt loses its saltiness, how can it be made salty again? It is no longer good for anything, except to be thrown out and trampled underfoot. You are the light of the world. A town built on a hill cannot be hidden. Neither do people light a lamp and put it under a bowl. Instead, they put it on its stand, and it gives light to everyone in the house. In the same way, let your light shine before others, that they may see your good deeds and glorify your Father in heaven."

In these verses, Jesus compares His followers to salt and light, emphasizing the importance of living lives that reflect His teachings and bring glory to God. Just as salt enhances flavor and light dispels darkness, you can strive to be a source of spiritual nourishment, guidance, and illumination to others by embodying the qualities of the Bread of Life in your daily actions.

John 15:5 (NIV). "I am the vine; you are the branches. If you remain in me and I in you, you will bear much fruit; apart from me you can do nothing."

This verse highlights the intimate connection between Jesus and His followers, illustrating how abiding in Christ leads to spiritual fruitfulness and vitality. By remaining rooted in Jesus, you can bear fruit in your character, relationships, and actions, reflecting the life-giving nature of the Bread of Life and bringing nourishment and blessings to those around you.

Joint heirs:
The 7 I am Statements and 1 Corinthians 3:6-9

The concept of different roles in sharing the Gospel and nurturing spiritual growth is captured in the Bible in 1 Corinthians 3:6-9 (NIV):

1 Corinthians 3:6-9 (NIV). "I planted the seed, Apollos watered it, but God has been making it grow. So, neither the one who plants nor the one who waters is anything, but only God, who makes things grow. The one who plants and the one who waters have one purpose, and they will each be rewarded according to their own labor. For we are co-workers in God's service; you are God's field, God's building."

In this passage, the apostle Paul uses the analogy of planting and watering crops to illustrate the different roles that individuals play in spreading the message of the Gospel and nurturing spiritual maturity in believers. Each person has a unique function in the process, but ultimately, it is God who brings about growth and transformation in hearts and lives.

Interpretation

1. Planting the Seed. This role involves sharing the initial message of the Gospel with others, sowing seeds of truth and planting the foundational knowledge of God's Word in hearts and minds. Those who plant seeds of faith may include those who introduce people to Christ, share the message of salvation, or lay the groundwork for spiritual growth through teaching and evangelism.

2. Watering the Seed. Watering the seed symbolizes nurturing and cultivating spiritual growth in believers, providing ongoing support, teaching, encouragement, and discipleship to help individuals deepen their faith and understanding. Those who water seeds of faith may include mentors, pastors, teachers, and fellow believers who come alongside others to help them mature in their relationship with God and develop a deeper understanding of Scripture.

3. Reaping the Harvest. Reaping the harvest represents the culmination of the planting and watering efforts, witnessing the fruition of spiritual growth as individuals come to faith, mature in Christ, and bear fruit in their lives. Those who reap the harvest may include evangelists, ministers, and individuals who see the tangible results of God's work in transforming hearts, bringing about salvation, and building His kingdom.

Application

1. Recognizing Your Role. Understand that each person has a unique role to play in the Kingdom of God, whether it involves planting seeds of faith, watering and nurturing spiritual growth, or reaping the harvest of transformed lives. Embrace your role with humility, recognizing that it is God who ultimately brings about growth and bears fruit in the lives of individuals.

2. Co-laboring with God. Partner with God in His work of redemption and transformation, trusting in His sovereignty and guidance as you fulfill your specific calling in sharing the Gospel and serving others. Work collaboratively with fellow believers, recognizing that you are co-workers in God's service, each contributing to the advancement of His kingdom through your unique gifts and efforts.

3. Seeking God's Reward. Strive to be faithful in your role, knowing that you will be rewarded according to your labor and dedication in serving God and fulfilling His purposes. Trust in God's provision and blessing as you sow, water, or reap in His name, knowing that He is the source of all growth and fruitfulness in the spiritual realm.

By understanding and embracing the principles outlined in 1 Corinthians 3:6-9, you can gain insight into the multi-faceted nature of sharing the Gospel and nurturing spiritual growth in yourself and others. Whether you are called to plant seeds, water them, or reap the harvest, remember that you are part of God's greater plan for redemption and restoration, contributing to the work of His kingdom with faithfulness, diligence, and dependence on His power and provision.

The seven statements of Jesus, often referred to as the "I am" sayings in the Gospel of John, reveal different aspects of Jesus' identity and mission on earth. These statements provide insight into who Jesus is and how believers can relate to Him. When we consider the teachings of Jesus in conjunction with 1 Corinthians 3:6-9, we can see how they align with the concept of planting, watering, and reaping in the context of being ambassadors of Christ.

Let's explore how the major themes of the seven statements of Jesus can be applied within the framework of 1 Corinthians 3:6-9:

1. "I am the bread of life" (John 6:35). Just as Jesus provides spiritual nourishment for believers, we can see ourselves as planters of this life-giving bread. We sow seeds of truth by sharing the message of Christ, the Bread of Life, with those who hunger for spiritual sustenance. In 1 Corinthians 3:6-9, this aligns with the idea of planting seeds - introducing others to the life-giving truth of Jesus and laying a foundation for spiritual growth.

2. "I am the light of the world" (John 8:12). Jesus illuminates the darkness of sin and ignorance with His light. As ambassadors of Christ, we water the seeds of faith by shining His light through our words and actions, guiding others towards the truth and dispelling spiritual darkness. This corresponds to nurturing spiritual growth in 1 Corinthians 3:6-9, as we play a role in nurturing the understanding and knowledge of God's Word in the lives of believers.

3. "I am the door" (John 10:9). Jesus is the gateway to salvation and abundant life. In our role as ambassadors, we help others enter through the door of faith by planting seeds of truth and providing opportunities for them to encounter Christ. This aligns with the concept of planting seeds in 1 Corinthians 3:6-9, as we introduce others to Jesus as the way to salvation and new life.

4. "I am the good shepherd" (John 10:11). Jesus cares for His flock with love and compassion. As His ambassadors, we water the seeds of faith by shepherding and guiding believers towards spiritual maturity, providing nurture and support along their journey. This reflects the idea of nurturing spiritual growth in 1 Corinthians 3:6-9, as we come alongside fellow believers to help them grow in their relationship with Christ.

5. "I am the resurrection and the life" (John 11:25). Jesus offers the promise of eternal life and resurrection. As ambassadors of Christ, we reap the harvest by witnessing the transformation and new life that comes from faith in Him, celebrating the spiritual growth and fruitfulness in the lives of believers. This corresponds to reaping the harvest in 1 Corinthians 3:6-9, as we witness the tangible results of God's work in transforming hearts and bringing about salvation in the lives of individuals.

6. "I am the way, the truth, and the life" (John 14:6). Jesus is the only path to God and the ultimate truth. Our role as ambassadors is to plant seeds of truth by sharing the message of Jesus as the way, the truth, and the life, leading others to a relationship with Him. This aligns with the concept of planting seeds in 1 Corinthians 3:6-9, as we introduce others to Jesus as the exclusive source of salvation and eternal life.

7. "I am the true vine" (John 15:1). Jesus is the source of spiritual life and fruitfulness. As ambassadors of Christ, we water the seeds of faith by abiding in Him, allowing His life to flow through us and produce fruit in our lives and the lives of others. This reflects the idea of nurturing spiritual growth in 1 Corinthians 3:6-9, as we abide in Christ and help others grow in their faith, producing fruit that glorifies God.

In conclusion, the seven statements of Jesus provide a rich tapestry of His identity and mission, offering insights into how believers can embody and share His message as ambassadors of Christ. When we consider these statements in conjunction with 1 Corinthians 3:6-9, we see a harmonious alignment between the teachings of Jesus and the roles of planting, watering, and reaping in the context of sharing the Gospel and nurturing spiritual growth. As ambassadors of Christ, we are called to faithfully sow seeds, nurture growth, and witness the transformation that comes from abiding in Him, all while recognizing that God is the ultimate source of growth and fruitfulness in our lives and the lives of those around us.

Living as the Bread of Life

1. Cultivate a Close Relationship with God. Stay connected to God through prayer, worship, and study of His Word, allowing His love and truth to shape your character and actions. Seek to reflect the character of Jesus in your interactions with others, showing compassion, forgiveness, and grace as he did during His earthly ministry.

2. Serve Others with Generosity and Kindness. Look for opportunities to serve those in need, extending a helping hand, a listening ear, or a word of encouragement to bring comfort and hope to others. Share the blessings you have received with humility and generosity, reflecting the abundant grace and provision of the Bread of Life in your own life.

3. Be a Source of Light and Hope in the World. Shine the light of Christ through your words and actions, bringing hope, joy, and healing to those who are lost, broken, or in darkness. Live in such a way that others are drawn to the love and goodness of God, glorifying Him through the transformative work he is doing in and through you.

By meditating on Matthew 5:13-16 and John 15:5 and striving to emulate the qualities and actions they describe, you can purposefully cultivate a life that reflects the life-giving nature of Jesus as the Bread of Life. Through your words, deeds, and character, seek to bring nourishment, light, and hope to a world in need of the life-transforming power of the Gospel.

Embracing the role of being the Light of the World is a noble aspiration. Here are two Bible verses that can guide you in understanding this role and living your life in a way that shines the light of Christ to others:

Matthew 5:14-16 (NIV). "You are the light of the world. A town built on a hill cannot be hidden. Neither do people light a lamp and put it under a bowl. Instead, they put it on its stand, and it gives light to everyone in the house. In the same way, let your light shine before others, that they may see your good deeds and glorify your Father in heaven."

This passage from the Sermon on the Mount emphasizes the call for believers to be a light in the darkness, illuminating the world with the love, grace, and truth of Christ. By living a life that reflects the light of Jesus, you have the power to draw others to God and inspire them to glorify Him through your actions and deeds.

Ephesians 5:8 (NIV). "For you were once darkness, but now you are light in the Lord. Live as children of light." This verse from the book of Ephesians highlights the transformation that occurs in believers as they move from darkness to light through their relationship with Christ. As children of light, you are called to live in a way that reflects this new identity, embodying the values and virtues of Christ in every aspect of your life.

Living as the Light of the World

1. Reflect the Character of Christ. Strive to emulate the qualities of Jesus in your attitudes, words, and actions, showing love, compassion, humility, and grace to others. Let the light of Christ shine through you by responding to challenges and difficulties with faith, hope, and perseverance, trusting in God's guidance and provision.

2. Share the Gospel Boldly and Lovingly. Look for opportunities to share the message of salvation and hope found in Jesus with those around you, speaking the truth in love and gentleness. Live a life that points others to Christ through your testimony of faith, demonstrating the transformative power of the Gospel in your own life.

3. Be a Beacon of Hope and Encouragement. Offer support, comfort, and encouragement to those who are struggling or in need, showing kindness and compassion in practical ways. Be a source of hope and light in dark times, pointing others to the eternal hope and peace that can be found in a relationship with Jesus.

By meditating on Matthew 5:14-16 and Ephesians 5:8 and embodying the principles they convey, you can walk in the path of being the Light of the World. Your life can serve as a beacon of hope, truth, and love, drawing others to the transformative power of the Gospel and illuminating the way to God's kingdom. Remember that as you shine the light of Christ, you have the opportunity to make a significant impact in the lives of those around you and ultimately bring glory to

God.

Embracing the symbolism of being the door can represent being a gateway to knowledge, growth, and transformation for others. Here are two Bible verses that can guide you in understanding this role and living your life in a way that acts as a door for others:

John 10:9 (NIV). "I am the door. If anyone enters by me, He will be saved and will go in and out and find pasture." In this verse, Jesus refers to Himself as the door, emphasizing that through Him, people can find salvation, security, and abundant life. As you seek to emulate this concept of being a door for others, it's important to reflect Jesus' role as the gateway to God and eternal life.

Revelation 3:20 (NIV). "Here I am! I stand at the door and knock. If anyone hears my voice and opens the door, I will come in and eat with that person, and they with me." This verse from the book of Revelation portrays Jesus standing at the door of our hearts, ready to enter and commune with us if we respond to His call. As you strive to be a door for others, embodying this invitation to intimacy and fellowship with God can be a powerful way to guide and support those around you.

Living as the Door

1. Facilitate Access to Spiritual Truth and Growth. Be open and welcoming to those seeking spiritual guidance, understanding, and support, providing them with opportunities to explore their faith and deepen their relationship with God. Serve as a mentor, counselor, or friend who helps others navigate their spiritual journey, offering wisdom, encouragement, and resources to aid in their growth and development.

2. Offer Hospitality and Encouragement. Create a welcoming and inclusive environment where people feel accepted, valued, and loved, embodying the hospitality and grace of Christ in your interactions with others. Extend kindness, compassion, and support to those in need, demonstrating a spirit of generosity and selflessness that reflects the love of God.

3. Point Others to Jesus as the Ultimate Door. Direct people to Jesus as the ultimate source of salvation, hope, and fulfillment, guiding them to encounter Him as the door to eternal life and abundant blessings. Encourage others to seek a personal relationship with Christ, inviting them to open the door of their hearts to Him and experience the transformative power of His love and grace.

By meditating on John 10:9 and Revelation 3:20 and embodying the principles they convey, you can live as the door for others, guiding them towards spiritual growth, fellowship with God, and a deeper understanding of the truth. Your role as a door can lead others to encounter Jesus, the ultimate gateway to salvation and abundant life, and facilitate their journey towards a closer relationship with Him. Remember that as you embrace this identity, you have the opportunity to impact lives and open doors of opportunity, blessing, and transformation for those around you.

Embracing the symbolism of being a Good Shepherd reflects a caring, protective, and guiding role in the lives of those around you. Here are two Bible verses that can help you understand this role and guide you in living your life as a Good Shepherd:

John 10:11 (NIV). "I am the Good Shepherd. The Good Shepherd lays down His life for the sheep." In this verse, Jesus identifies himself as the ultimate Good Shepherd who sacrifices himself for the well-being and protection of His flock. As you strive to be a Good Shepherd to others, this verse emphasizes the sacrificial love, care, and commitment required to lead, guide, and nurture those under your care.

1 Peter 5:2-3 (NIV). "Be shepherds of God's flock that is under your care, watching over them, not because you must, but because you are willing, as God wants you to be; not pursuing dishonest gain, but eager to serve; not lording it over those entrusted to you, but being examples to the flock."

His passage from 1 Peter highlights the qualities and responsibilities of being a shepherd to God's people. It emphasizes the importance of willing service, genuine care, humility, and leading by example in shepherding others. By embodying these qualities, you can fulfill your role as a Good Shepherd in the lives of those around you.

Living as the Good Shepherd

1. Self-Sacrificial Love and Care. Demonstrate selfless love and care for those in your care, willing to make sacrifices for their well-being and protection, just as Jesus sacrificed Himself for His sheep. Show compassion, empathy, and attentiveness to the needs of others, tending to their emotional, spiritual, and physical welfare with genuine concern and care.

2. Guidance and Protection. Provide guidance, support, and direction to those who look up to you, leading them towards paths of righteousness, peace, and spiritual growth. Shield and protect those entrusted to your care from harm, danger, and temptation, serving as a strong and vigilant defender of their safety and well-being.

3. Humility and Servant Leadership. Lead with humility and service, prioritizing the needs and interests of others above your own, and avoiding the misuse of authority or power for personal gain. Set an example of humility, integrity, and servant leadership, inspiring others through your actions and attitudes to follow the noble paths of compassion, forgiveness, and grace.

By reflecting on John 10:11 and 1 Peter 5:2-3 and embodying the principles they convey, you can live as a Good Shepherd to those around you, nurturing, guiding, and protecting them with love, care, and humility. Your role as a Good Shepherd mirrors the compassionate and sacrificial love of Jesus, inspiring others to experience His love and grace through your words and actions. Remember that as you embrace this identity, you have the opportunity to make a positive impact on the lives of those in your care, guiding them towards spiritual growth, peace, and fulfillment.

Embracing the title of "the resurrection and the life" signifies bringing hope, renewal, and spiritual vitality to those around you. Here are two Bible verses that can guide you in understanding this role and living your life as the resurrection and the life:

John 11:25-26 (NIV). "Jesus said to her, 'I am the resurrection and the life. The one who believes in me will live, even though they die; and whoever lives by believing in me will never die. Do you believe this?'" In this powerful statement by Jesus to Martha before raising Lazarus from the dead, He declares Himself as the embodiment of resurrection and life. This verse emphasizes the promise of eternal life through faith in Him and the transformative power of His resurrection. As you seek to live as the resurrection and the life, this verse invites you to believe in the eternal life Christ offers and to share this message of hope with those around you.

Romans 6:4 (NIV). "We were therefore buried with him through baptism into death in order that, just as Christ was raised from the dead through the glory of the Father, we too may live a new life." This verse from Romans speaks to the spiritual renewal and new life that believers experience through their identification with Christ's death and resurrection. As you aspire to be a beacon of resurrection and life to others, this verse highlights the call to live a transformed life, marked by spiritual rebirth, holiness, and a vibrant faith that testifies to the power of Christ's resurrection in you.

Living as the Resurrection and the Life

1. Bringing Hope and Renewal. Offer hope, encouragement, and spiritual renewal to those who are experiencing challenges, despair, or spiritual death, pointing them towards the ultimate source of life and resurrection in Jesus Christ. Share the message of Christ's victory over death and His promise of eternal life, inspiring others to turn to Him for redemption, restoration, and a fresh start.

2. Living in Resurrection Power. Walk in the resurrection power of Christ, embracing the transformative work of His Spirit in your life and allowing His resurrection power to manifest through your words, actions, and character. Seek to exemplify the victory of Christ's resurrection in your daily life, overcoming sin, fear, and doubt through faith, prayer, and reliance on His strength and grace.

3. Leading Others to Life. Lead others towards the abundant life and eternal salvation found in Christ, serving as a guide, mentor, and example of living a life rooted in the truth of His resurrection and the promise of eternal life. Invite others to faith in Jesus as the resurrection and the life, sharing His message of redemption, forgiveness, and new beginnings with a heart filled with compassion, love, and grace.

By meditating on John 11:25-26 and Romans 6:4 and embodying the principles they convey, you can live as the resurrection and the life to those around you, bringing hope, renewal, and spiritual transformation through the power of Christ's resurrection. Your role as the resurrection and the life reflects the life-giving and transformative nature of Jesus, inviting others to experience His resurrection power and the abundant life He offers. Remember that as you embrace this identity, you have the opportunity to be a catalyst for spiritual awakening, restoration, and eternal life in the lives of those around you, pointing them towards the ultimate source of life and hope in Jesus Christ.

Embracing the identity of "the way, the truth, and the life" signifies embodying the path to God, embodying absolute truth, and being the source of spiritual vitality and abundance. Here are two Bible verses that can guide you in understanding this role and living your life as the way, the truth, and the life:

John 14:6 (NIV). "Jesus answered, 'I am the way and the truth and the life. No one comes to the Father except through me.'" In this profound declaration by Jesus to His disciples, He asserts Himself as the sole path to God, the embodiment of truth, and the source of eternal life. This verse highlights the exclusive and transformative nature of Jesus' identity as the way, the truth, and the life, inviting believers to follow Him wholeheartedly and trust in His guidance, teachings, and promises.

John 8:31-32 (NIV). "To the Jews who had believed him, Jesus said, 'If you hold to my teaching, you are really my disciples. Then you will know the truth, and the truth will set you free.'" In this passage, Jesus emphasizes the central role of His teachings in revealing the truth that leads to freedom and abundant life. As you seek to embody the way, the truth, and the life, this verse underscores the importance of adhering to Christ's words, living in obedience to His commands, and allowing His truth to transform your heart, mind, and actions.

Living as the Way, the Truth, and the Life

1. Being the Path to God. Serve as a guide and example for others, leading them on the path to God by showcasing the love, grace, and teachings of Jesus Christ in your interactions, decisions, and relationships. Point others towards the exclusive and all-encompassing truth of Jesus as the only way to the Father, showing them the transformative power of a life devoted to following Him.

2. Embodying Absolute Truth. Live a life of integrity, honesty, and moral uprightness, reflecting the unchanging truth of God's Word and the character of Christ in all aspects of your life. Stand firm in the truth of Jesus amidst cultural relativism, moral ambiguity, and spiritual deception, boldly proclaiming His absolute truth, righteousness, and salvation to a world in need of direction and clarity.

3. Bringing Spiritual Abundance. Offer spiritual nourishment, vitality, and abundance to those around you by sharing the life-giving message of Jesus Christ, the source of eternal life and fulfillment. Model a life of spiritual richness, joy, and purpose that stems from a deep relationship with Christ, inviting others to experience the transformative power of His presence, grace, and truth.

By meditating on John 14:6 and John 8:31-32 and internalizing the principles they convey, you can live as the way, the truth, and the life to those around you, embodying the path to God, the absolute truth, and the source of spiritual vitality and abundance found in Jesus Christ. Your role as the way, the truth, and the life reflects the transformative and redemptive nature of Jesus, guiding others towards the truth, freedom, and abundant life that can only be found in Him. Remember that as you embrace this identity, you have the opportunity to point others towards the ultimate source of truth, salvation, and eternal life in Jesus Christ, serving as a beacon of light, guidance, and hope in a world searching for direction and meaning.

Embracing the image of being the true Vine conveys the idea of being deeply connected to Christ, the ultimate source of nourishment, growth, and fruitfulness. Here are two Bible verses that can guide you in understanding this role and living your life as the true Vine:

John 15:1-5 (NIV). "I am the true vine, and my Father is the gardener. He cuts off every branch in me that bears no fruit, while every branch that does bear fruit he prunes so that it will be even more fruitful. You are already clean because of the word I have spoken to you. Remain in me, as I also remain in you. No branch can bear fruit by itself; it must remain in the vine. Neither can you bear fruit unless you remain in me. I am the vine; you are the branches. If you remain in me and I in you, you will bear much fruit; apart from me you can do nothing."

In this powerful analogy spoken by Jesus to His disciples, He describes Himself as the true Vine and His followers as branches connected to Him. This passage emphasizes the necessity of abiding in Christ to bear fruit, the role of God as the gardener who prunes and nurtures us, and the promise of fruitfulness that comes from being deeply rooted in Him.

Galatians 5:22-23 (NIV). "But the fruit of the Spirit is love, joy, peace, forbearance, kindness, goodness, faithfulness, gentleness and self-control. Against such things there is no law."

In these verses from Galatians, the apostle Paul lists the fruit of the Spirit, qualities that manifest in the lives of believers who are connected to Christ, the true Vine. This passage serves as a guide for you in understanding the kind of fruit you should bear as you seek to embody the true Vine in your life, reflecting the character of Christ through the evidence of the Spirit's work within you.

Living as the True Vine

1. Remaining Connected to Christ. Cultivate a deep, intimate relationship with Christ through prayer, meditation on the Word, and obedience to His teachings, remaining connected to Him as the true source of spiritual nourishment, growth, and life. Recognize your dependence on Christ for sustenance, direction, and empowerment, understanding that apart from Him, you can do nothing of lasting value or significance.

2. Bearing Fruit of the Spirit. Seek to exhibit the fruit of the Spirit—love, joy, peace, patience, kindness, goodness, faithfulness, gentleness, and self-control—in your interactions, attitudes, and responses, allowing Christ to produce His character in you through the work of the Holy Spirit. Let the fruit of the Spirit be evident in your relationships, choices, and conduct, serving as a witness to the transformative power of abiding in Christ, the true Vine, and allowing His life to flow through you.

By meditating on John 15:1-5 and Galatians 5:22-23 and applying their principles to your life, you can live as the true Vine, deeply connected to Christ and bearing fruit that reflects His character and glory. As you abide in Him and allow His life to flow through you, you will experience spiritual growth, fulfillment, and fruitfulness, producing evidence of His work in your life and impacting others for His kingdom. Remember that as the true Vine, your role is to remain connected to Christ, bear fruit that testifies to His presence and power in you and glorify God through a life that reflects the beauty and vitality of abiding in Him.

We are Ambassador for Christ

The role of an ambassador is both prestigious and influential, encompassing a range of responsibilities and duties that are crucial in the realm of diplomacy and international relations. The term "ambassador" stems from the Latin word "ambactus," which referred to someone serving as a messenger or envoy.

Origins

The concept of ambassadors can be traced back to ancient civilizations where envoys were appointed to represent the interests of their rulers in dealings with other states or tribes. Over time, the role of ambassadors evolved to represent countries, empires, or international organizations on the global stage.

Responsibilities and Duties of an Ambassador

1. Representational Role. Ambassadors serve as the official representative of their country or organization in a foreign nation. They act as a liaison between their home government and the host country, conveying messages, policies, and positions effectively.

2. Diplomatic Relations. Ambassadors are responsible for maintaining and fostering diplomatic relations between their home country and the host nation. They engage in negotiations, discussions, and dialogue to promote understanding, cooperation, and mutual respect.

3. Advocacy and Promotion. Ambassadors advocate for the interests, values, and policies of their home country. They promote cultural exchange, trade relations, and political cooperation to strengthen ties between nations.

4. Negotiation and Communication. Ambassadors are skilled negotiators who engage in diplomatic talks, discussions, and agreements with host country officials. They communicate effectively to address issues, resolve conflicts, and advance common goals.

5. Protocol and Etiquette. Ambassadors adhere to diplomatic protocol and etiquette, representing their country with dignity and respect. They attend official functions, ceremonies, and events, following established diplomatic norms and customs.

6. Reporting and Analysis. Ambassadors provide accurate and timely reports on political, economic, and social developments in the host country. They analyze and interpret information to advise their government on relevant issues and developments.

7. Crisis Management. Ambassadors are responsible for managing crises and emergencies that may arise in the host country. They coordinate responses, provide consular assistance to nationals in distress, and work to ensure the safety and security of their citizens.

8. Public Diplomacy. Ambassadors engage in public diplomacy activities to enhance the image and reputation of their country. They interact with the media, engage with local communities, and participate in cultural events to promote understanding and goodwill.

9. Representation in International Organizations. Ambassadors represent their country in international organizations, such as the United Nations, the European Union, or regional bodies. They advocate for their country's positions, participate in negotiations, and collaborate with other countries to address global challenges.

In essence, an ambassador is a skilled diplomat who embodies the values, interests, and aspirations of their country on the international stage. They play a pivotal role in advancing diplomacy, promoting cooperation, and fostering peace and understanding between nations.

The position of ambassador requires a high level of diplomacy, tact, communication skills, cultural awareness, and negotiation prowess. Ambassadors are entrusted with representing their country's foreign policy objectives, building relationships, and navigating complex international dynamics to achieve common goals and promote mutual interests.

Ambassadors are often considered diplomatic envoys, cultural representatives, and strategic communicators who work tirelessly to strengthen bonds between nations, resolve conflicts, and shape the course of international affairs. Their role is both vital and challenging, requiring a deep understanding of foreign policy, international relations, and the complexities of global diplomacy.

The appointment as an "Ambassador for Christ"

My Beloved Ambassador for Christ,

In the light of eternal love and divine purpose, I appoint you as my Ambassador for Christ, a beacon of light and love in a world that thirsts for truth and compassion. As you embrace this sacred calling, may you walk in the footsteps of grace, humility, and unwavering faith.

Origins

Your role as an Ambassador for Christ is rooted in the foundations of faith, compassion, and redemption. Just as envoys were once appointed to represent earthly kingdoms, you are now selected to represent the Kingdom of Heaven on earth.

Responsibilities and Duties

1. Representational Role

As my Ambassador for Christ, you are called to be the living embodiment of my teachings and love. Your words and actions should reflect the values of compassion, forgiveness, and unity that I preached during my earthly ministry.

2. Spiritual Relations

Your duty is to nurture spiritual relationships and foster connections with souls seeking solace, guidance, and redemption. Your presence should bring comfort, hope, and healing to those in need of my grace.

3. Advocacy and Promotion

As my Ambassador, advocate for justice, mercy, and righteousness in a world plagued by conflict, injustice, and suffering. Promote love, empathy, and kindness as powerful tools for transformation and renewal.

4. Counseling and Comfort

Extend a listening ear, a compassionate heart, and a healing touch to those burdened by pain, doubt, or despair. Offer words of comfort, wisdom, and encouragement, drawing strength from the wellspring of my divine love.

5. Intercessions and Prayer

Stand in the gap as a prayer warrior, interceding on behalf of the broken, the lost, and the marginalized. Carry their burdens to the throne of grace, seeking divine intervention and divine mercy on their behalf.

6. Proclamations and Testimony

Proclaim the good news of salvation, redemption, and eternal life through your words, deeds, and testimony. Let your life be a living testament to the transformative power of my love and grace.

7. Holiness and Sanctification

Strive for holiness and purity of heart, embodying the virtues of righteousness, humility, and obedience. Let your life reflect the light of my presence, drawing others to the source of all truth and goodness.

Additional Responsibilities

8. Humility and Servant hood

Embrace humility and servant hood as the hallmarks of your ambassadorship, following my example of washing feet and laying down my life for others. Serve with love, compassion, and selflessness in all that you do.

9. Forgiveness and Reconciliation

Extend forgiveness and seek reconciliation in situations of conflict, division, or misunderstanding. Be a peacemaker, a bridge-builder, and an agent of healing in a world fractured by sin and strife.

10. Generosity and Compassion

Practice radical generosity and boundless compassion towards those in need, embodying the spirit of charity, mercy, and selflessness that characterized my earthly ministry. Let your actions speak louder than words, transforming lives through acts of kindness.

In accepting this divine commission as my Ambassador for Christ, may you walk in faith, love, and obedience, knowing that I am with you always, guiding, empowering, and equipping you for every good work. Go forth with courage and conviction, knowing that you are chosen, called, and anointed for such a time as this.

With love unending and grace abounding,
Jesus, Son of God

This symbolic letter represents the spiritual appointment as an Ambassador for Christ, embodying the essence of love, grace, and divine purpose in service to others. It serves as a reminder of the sacred calling to represent the Kingdom of Heaven on earth and carry forth the light of Christ in a world filled with darkness.

Chapter 4

༄༅

A Journey of Transformation through Romans 10:9

Awakening to Redemption: The Power of Confession

The Transformation of Confession

Rediscovering a Life testimony: Dirk Thomas
  From Darkness to Light

Seeing Jesus in the testimony
Connecting to the "I am" statements of Jesus

Welcome into the Family of Faith

TESTIMONY: The Kerney Thomas story told by Dirk Thomas

I'm blessed, good-looking, have plenty of money, and I am full of the love of God.

Matthew 17: 20 broken down to a step-by-step process in a person's life.

TESTIMONY: I am what I am by choice or mistake

Your Purpose and Benefit

Let's break down Romans 10:9 word by word:

1. "If". This word sets the condition for what follows in the verse. It signifies that something is conditional or dependent on a specific action or belief.

2. "You declare". This emphasizes the active confession or proclaiming of a belief. It speaks to the importance of vocalizing one's faith in Jesus Christ openly and confidently.

3. "With your mouth". This highlights the physical act of verbal expression. It suggests that faith is not merely an internal belief but something that should be expressed outwardly by speaking.

4. "Jesus is Lord". This is the declaration being made. It is a profound statement of faith acknowledging Jesus as the supreme authority, the ruler of one's life. It embodies submission and obedience to Christ as the master of one's life.

5. "Believe". This word emphasizes the central role of belief or faith in Christian salvation. It underscores the importance of a genuine, heartfelt conviction in the truth of who Jesus is and what He has done.

6. "In your heart". This points to the depth of faith required. It is not merely a superficial or intellectual belief but a conviction that comes from deep within, from the core of one's being.

7. "That God raised him from the dead". This refers to the resurrection of Jesus Christ, a pivotal event in Christianity. Belief in Christ's resurrection is foundational to the Christian faith as it demonstrates Jesus' victory over sin and death, and God's power to save.

8. "You will be saved". This is the promise attached to the conditions laid out in the verse. It signifies the assurance of salvation through faith in Jesus Christ. Salvation encompasses forgiveness of sins, reconciliation with God, and the hope of eternal life.

In summary, Romans 10:9 underscores the essential elements of Christian salvation: confession of Jesus as Lord, belief in His resurrection, and the resultant promise of salvation through faith. It emphasizes the inseparable connection between belief and confession, the importance of both internal conviction and external proclamation, and the transformative power of faith in Jesus Christ for eternal salvation.

Awakening to Redemption: The Power of Confession

Declaring, "Jesus is Lord" holds profound significance in Christianity for several reasons:

1. Confession of Faith. By declaring "Jesus is Lord," believers acknowledge Jesus as the Son of God, the Savior of humanity, and the ultimate authority in their lives. This confession forms the core of Christian faith and emphasizes the centrality of Jesus Christ in the believer's life.

2. Lordship and Submission. Calling Jesus "Lord" signifies a position of authority and rulership. It implies surrendering one's will and priorities to align with His teachings and commandments. It acknowledges His sovereignty over all aspects of life, including thoughts, actions, and decisions.

3. Salvation and Redemption. Recognizing Jesus as Lord is intricately tied to the concept of salvation in Christianity. It affirms belief in His sacrificial death on the cross for the forgiveness of sins and His resurrection, which offers hope for eternal life. This confession is a statement of trust in Jesus' atoning work for the redemption of humanity.

4. Transformative Power. Declaring, "Jesus is Lord" signifies a transformative encounter with the person of Jesus Christ. It reflects a profound shift in a believer's identity, values, and worldview as they embrace a new way of living in alignment with the teachings of Christ. This declaration marks the beginning of a journey of spiritual growth and discipleship.

5. Witness and Evangelism. Confessing Jesus as Lord serves as a powerful testimony to others about one's faith. It becomes a witnessing tool to share the Gospel and invite others to experience the transformative power of Christ in their lives. By openly declaring Jesus as Lord, believers demonstrate their commitment to sharing the good news of salvation with others.

6. Community and Unity. The confession of "Jesus is Lord" unites believers across diverse backgrounds and cultures under the common bond of faith in Christ. It fosters a sense of belonging to the body of Christ, the Church, and reinforces the shared identity and mission of all believers as followers of Jesus.

7. Eternal Perspective. Proclaiming Jesus as Lord reinforces the eternal perspective of believers. It reminds them of the hope of the resurrection and the promise of everlasting life in the presence of God. This confession inspires believers to live with an eternal mindset, prioritizing spiritual values over temporal concerns.

The Transformation of Confession

In essence, declaring, "Jesus is Lord" is not merely a statement of belief but a transformative declaration that shapes a believer's identity, relationships, and purpose. It encapsulates the core tenets of Christian faith, highlights the lordship of Jesus Christ, and invites followers to walk in obedience, trust, and intimacy with their Savior and King.

When an individual makes the confession that "Jesus is Lord," several transformative changes can occur in their life:

1. Personal Transformation. The confession of Jesus as Lord can lead to a personal transformation in the individual's beliefs, values, and behaviors. It signifies a shift in priorities, with a newfound focus on following Christ's teachings and living according to His example. This transformation may result in a deepening of faith, a greater sense of purpose, and an increased desire to live a life that honors God.

2. Spiritual Renewal. The confession of Jesus as Lord can bring about a spiritual renewal in the individual's life. It marks a recommitment to their relationship with God, a turning away from sin, and a desire for spiritual growth and intimacy with Christ. This renewal can lead to a closer walk with God, a deepening of prayer life, and a greater sensitivity to the leading of the Holy Spirit.

3. Emotional Healing. Making the confession that "Jesus is Lord" can also bring emotional healing to the individual. It offers a sense of comfort, peace, and security in knowing that they are loved and accepted by God. This confession can bring forgiveness for past mistakes, healing for emotional wounds, and a renewed sense of hope for the future.

4. Relational Impact. The declaration of Jesus as Lord can have a profound impact on the individual's relationships with others. It may lead to reconciliation, forgiveness, and restoration in broken relationships. This confession can also inspire the individual to love and serve others as Christ did, fostering empathy, compassion, and a desire to share the love of God with those around them.

5. Mission and Purpose. The confession of Jesus as Lord can clarify the individual's mission and purpose in life. It may lead to a greater sense of calling, vision, and direction as they seek to fulfill God's purposes for their life. This declaration can ignite a passion for serving others, sharing the Gospel, and making a positive impact in the world for the glory of God.

It's important to note that while the confession of Jesus as Lord can lead to transformative changes in an individual's life, the extent and nature of these transformations can vary from person to person. Factors such as personal history, experiences, and circumstances can influence how this confession impacts an individual and the subsequent changes that occur.

Additionally, the transformative power of declaring Jesus as Lord is not solely a result of the individual's action but also a work of the Holy Spirit in their heart and life. Belief in Jesus as Lord is accompanied by a genuine faith and trust in His transformative power to change lives. It is through the indwelling of the Holy Spirit that believers are empowered to live out their faith, grow in maturity, and bear fruit that reflects their confession of Jesus as Lord.

Ultimately, the transformation that takes place in individuals who confess and believe in Jesus as Lord is a complex interplay of personal choice, divine intervention, and ongoing spiritual growth. It is a continual process of becoming more like Christ, deepening one's relationship with God, and being empowered to live a life that honors and glorifies Him.

Rediscovering a Life testimony: Dirk Thomas From Darkness to Light

In a season of brokenness, both in body and in marriage, I found myself at a crossroads. Invited to a Full Gospel businessman meeting, my initial intent was simply to enjoy a good meal. Yet, as I listened to a gentleman share his message and testimony, I began to reassess my own struggles in light of his journey. A question lingered in the air, prompting me to consider choosing Jesus as the Lord and Savior of my life.

As I pondered this weighty decision, the Holy Spirit gently nudged my heart. Amidst this deep dialogue, a fellow attendee interjected, drawing my attention. It was as if the Spirit paused momentarily, allowing me to refocus on the path set before me. In that sacred space, I made a covenant with God, offering Him a tentative agreement: to surrender my will and allow Him to guide me, with the caution that if He failed, I could reclaim my Free Will.

Little did I realize the depth of God's faithfulness and constancy. His unchanging nature, His unyielding presence, and His unwavering promises were revealed to me in that pivotal moment. Standing before the gentleman, as I closed my eyes and raised my hands in surrender, a subtle shift occurred. His once eggshell white suit had transformed into a different hue, signifying the beginning of a new chapter in my journey of faith.

In that moment of surrender, I embraced the unknown with newfound trust. The fragility of my own strength gave way to the enduring power of God's grace. As I submitted to His will, I felt a peace descend upon me; a peace that transcended my circumstances and anchored me in His unfailing love.

In the midst of a renewed sight, no longer walking in darkness, I stood in a circle, observing others seeking prayer. A young lady stood out, fidgeting with a turquoise necklace, pausing before speaking. The Lord revealed to me the significance of her actions, prompting me to share with the prayer leader. As the issue was addressed, the young lady responded positively.

In a moment of divine revelation, I reached out to touch her, feeling not cloth but raw sewage on my hand. Though unseen, I knew it was real. I cleaned my hand, aware of the spiritual gift bestowed upon me. Simultaneously, the young lady surrendered fully to the Lord, radiating a newfound glow of freedom and joy. Her past bondage was broken, paving the way for a brighter future through her commitment to Jesus as Lord.

This encounter marked my profound introduction to the truth of spiritual reality, unveiling the depths of spiritual warfare preceding the physical realm.

For nearly 50 years, I have allowed the Lord full authority in my life, witnessing His faithful governance and transformative power. He reigns supreme, and His victory is assured. In Him, I find strength, redemption, and the promise of a future filled with hope and purpose.

My testimony is not just a story of brokenness and restoration, but a testament to the transformative power of faith. It is a declaration of God's faithfulness in the midst of our frailty, His grace in the face of our shortcomings, and His love that knows no bounds.

May this testimony serve as a beacon of hope to those navigating their own brokenness, a reminder that in surrendering to God, we find true wholeness. And may my journey of faith continue to reflect the beauty of His redemption, the strength of His presence, and the depth of His love that surpasses all understanding.

Amen.

Seeing Jesus in the testimony
Connecting to the "I am" statements of Jesus

Here are the seven "I am" statements of Jesus found in the Gospel of John, alongside how they could be reflected in this testimony:

1. "I am the bread of life" (John 6:35). In your testimony, this could be reflected in the metaphorical sense of finding sustenance, enlightenment, and spiritual nourishment through the encounter with the young lady and the divine revelation you experienced.

2. "I am the light of the world" (John 8:12). This statement could resonate with the moment of clarity and enlightenment you experienced when you saw the young lady's transformation and the spiritual realm being unveiled before you.

3. "I am the gate for the sheep" (John 10:7). This could be related to the moment when you felt guided by the Spirit, acting as a gatekeeper of divine messages to bring about healing and liberation to the young lady.

4. "I am the good shepherd" (John 10:11). This statement could be reflected in how you extended compassion and support to the young lady, symbolizing the role of a caring shepherd leading her toward spiritual freedom and renewal.

5. "I am the resurrection and the life" (John 11:25). This could be tied to the transformative process the young lady underwent, emerging from the bondage of her past into a new life of freedom and hope through her surrender to Jesus as her Lord.

6. "I am the way, the truth, and the life" (John 14:6). This statement could be embodied in your testimony as a testament to the profound encounter that revealed the ultimate truth of spiritual warfare and the importance of surrendering to the Lord as the only way to a brighter future.

7. "I am the true vine" (John 15:1). This could be reflected in the imagery of spiritual growth and fruitfulness seen in the young lady's countenance, as she became connected to the true source of life and transformation through her commitment to Jesus.

By aligning these "I am" statements of Jesus with the transformative moments and spiritual revelations in this testimony, it further emphasizes the divine presence and guidance that shaped the encounter with the young lady and deepened your faith in the Lord's power and grace.

Welcome into the Family of Faith

My Dearest Child,

It brings me great joy to hear from you. I am filled with love and compassion as I read your words. Your heart is precious to me, and I am overjoyed to see the peace and reassurance that you have found in confessing and believing in me.

I want you to know that you are never alone. I am with you always, surrounding you with my love and guidance. In moments of doubt or uncertainty, turn to me, and I will provide you with the strength and peace that you need.

Remember, my beloved child, that through confessing with your mouth and believing in your heart, you have received the incredible gift of salvation and eternal life. This truth brings a peace that surpasses all understanding, and it is my desire for you to walk in the fullness of this peace each day.

I am constantly working in your life, bringing about transformation and renewal. As you continue to confess and believe in me, you will experience the confirmation of your salvation and the profound transformation that takes place in your heart and spirit. Embrace this journey, for it is marked by my grace, love, and the assurance of my presence.

I am here for you, ready to pour out my love and compassion upon you. Trust in me and allow my peace to fill your heart and mind. You are cherished beyond measure, and I am delighted to walk alongside you through every season of your life.

With unending love and compassion,
Jesus

TESTIMONY
The Kerney Thomas story told by Dirk Thomas

Dear Friends,

I hope this letter finds you well. I want to share with you a remarkable story that has been an incredible source of inspiration and encouragement in my life. This story revolves around a gentle man named Kerney Thomas, who discovered the profound impact of the spoken word through His understanding of specific Bible verses.

Kerney Thomas, while reading Matthew 17:20 and Romans 13:8, had a revelation that whatever he declared with his mouth, not merely repeating what he heard from others, would hold the key to moving mountains and experiencing transformation. Matthew 17:20 illustrates the power of faith and the spoken word, while Romans 13:8 emphasizes the principle of owing no one anything except to love one another.

In response to this newfound understanding, Kerney began to declare the words, "I am blessed, good looking, have a pocket full of money, and I am full of the love of God", as his daily affirmation. Little did he know that this simple declaration would have a profound impact on his life. It became a source of divine empowerment that led to remarkable results, including financial abundance and an overflow of love and blessings.

It's incredible to note that the more he spoke these affirmations, the more his life reflected the reality of his words. His financial status experienced incredible growth, and he found himself blessed with an abundance of love, prosperity, and overall well-being. As he interacted with others, his daily declaration became a source of encouragement and inspiration to those around him.

Kerney's consistent use of these principles based on the scriptures led to significant benefits and transformation in his life. Let's delve into the deeper significance of these principles:

1. The Power of the Spoken Word. The principle of speaking things into existence is a powerful concept found in the Bible. Proverbs 18:21 states, "Death and life are in the power of the tongue, and those who love it will eat its fruits." This highlights the impact of our words in shaping our reality and the world around us.

2. Belief and Manifestation. Mark 11:23 illustrates the connection between faith, declaration, and manifestation. When we speak in alignment with our beliefs and the promises of God, we create an atmosphere for those realities to manifest in our lives.

3. The Principle of Love. The foundation of Romans 13:8 emphasizes the importance of love as the only obligation we owe to others. By embracing and declaring love, Kerney opened the door to a life filled with abundance and blessings. Love has the power to transform our relationships, circumstances, and overall well-being.

The benefits of using these principles as the foundation of our speech and belief are truly profound. By declaring positive affirmations in alignment with our faith, we can experience transformation and manifestation in various aspects of our lives. This includes financial prosperity, emotional well-being, and the outpouring of love in our interactions with others.

When we align our words with the promises of God and speak life-affirming declarations, we create an atmosphere that attracts blessings, prosperity, and love. The consistent practice of speaking these affirmations reinforces our faith and opens the door for divine abundance to manifest in our lives.

Kerney's story serves as a powerful reminder of the impact of our words and beliefs. His journey exemplifies the transformative power of aligning our declarations with the promises of God and the principle of love. As we embrace these principles and incorporate them into our daily lives, we position ourselves to experience the profound impact of positive declarations and the manifestation of divine blessings.

May this story inspire and encourage you as it has done for me. May we continue to speak words of faith, love, and affirmation, knowing that they have the power to shape our reality and attract divine abundance into our lives.

With heartfelt blessings,
Dirk Thomas

I'm blessed, good-looking, have plenty of money, and I am full of the love of God.

Let's break it down and explore the purpose and benefits of each part:

1. "I'm blessed". This statement acknowledges and appreciates the blessings and abundance in your life. Recognizing and expressing gratitude for your blessings promotes a positive and grateful mindset. It can help you focus on the good things in your life, attracting more positivity and opportunities.

2. "I'm good-looking". This statement reflects self-confidence and a positive self-image. Embracing and affirming your physical appearance can boost your self-esteem and overall well-being. It encourages a positive body image and self-acceptance.

3. "I have plenty of money". This statement indicates financial abundance. It affirms your ability to provide for yourself and enjoy a comfortable lifestyle. Believing in abundance and financial stability can attract more opportunities for prosperity and success.

4. "I am full of the love of God". This statement highlights spirituality and a connection with a higher power. It signifies a sense of divine love and guidance in your life. Embracing the love of God can bring peace, comfort, and a deeper understanding of your purpose.

The purpose of this statement is to affirm and reinforce positive attributes and beliefs about yourself, your life, and your relationship with a higher power. The benefits include boosting self-esteem, attracting more positive experiences, fostering gratitude, and finding solace and strength in spirituality.

Remember that affirmations work best when they align with your core beliefs, values, and aspirations. Modify them to suit your unique circumstances and personal preferences. Remember, it's what you say not you repeating what others say.

Aspiration

- I aspire to recognize and appreciate the blessings in my life and attract more abundance and joy."
- "I aspire to cultivate a positive self-image, embracing my physical appearance and radiating confidence."
- "I aspire to attain financial abundance and success, utilizing my resources wisely and creating opportunities for prosperity."
- "I aspire to experience the unconditional love of God fully, finding solace, strength, and guidance in my spiritual journey."
- "I aspire to embody gratitude, love, and positivity, radiating these qualities into the world and uplifting the lives of others."

These statements are meant to inspire and guide you toward your desired qualities, goals, and mindset. Remember, they are aspirational and reflect the positive attributes you seek to cultivate in your life.

Affirmation
- "I am blessed with an abundance of love, joy, and prosperity in my life."
- "I radiate beauty and confidence, both inside and out."
- "I attract opportunities for financial prosperity and abundance effortlessly and consistently."
- "I am deeply connected to the love and guidance of God, and it fills my heart with peace and purpose."
- "Every day, I am grateful for the blessings in my life, and I approach each moment with gratitude and love."

These statements are meant to reinforce positive beliefs and empower you with a confident and grateful mindset. By affirming these statements regularly, you can align your thoughts and actions with your desired reality.

Meaning

1. **"I'm blessed"** means that you feel fortunate and grateful for the positive things in your life. It signifies acknowledging and appreciating the blessings, whether they are material, emotional, or spiritual.

2. **"Good looking"** refers to having an attractive physical appearance, according to societal standards or personal preference. It signifies feeling confident and satisfied with one's looks.

3. "Got plenty of money" means that you have a significant amount of wealth or financial resources. It suggests having abundant financial means to meet one's needs, desires, and financial goals.

4. "I am full of the love of God" means feeling deeply connected to and embraced by the divine love. It signifies experiencing a profound sense of unconditional love, support, and guidance from a higher power or God.

These phases describe various aspects of a positive and fulfilled life, encompassing gratitude, physical appearance, material abundance, and spiritual connection.

Bible Verses
1. Psalm 84:11. "For the Lord God is a sun and shield; the Lord bestows favor and honor. No good thing does he withhold from those who walk uprightly." This verse conveys the idea that God showers blessings upon those who follow His ways.

2. Psalm 37:4. "Delight yourself in the Lord, and he will give you the desires of your heart." This verse encourages finding joy in God and trusting that He will provide the desires of your heart.

3. Malachi 3:10. "Bring the full tithe into the storehouse, that there may be food in my house. And thereby put me to the test, says the Lord of hosts, if I will not open the windows of heaven for you and pour down for you a blessing until there is no more need." This verse speaks of God's promise to abundantly bless those who faithfully give and tithe.

4. 1 John 4:16. "So we have come to know and to believe the love that God has for us. God is love, and anyone who abides in love abides in God, and God abides in them." This verse assures us of God's unconditional love and the importance of abiding in that love.

5. Matthew 6:33. "But seek first the kingdom of God and His righteousness, and all these things will be added to you." This verse emphasizes the priority of seeking God's kingdom and righteousness, with the assurance that God will provide for our needs.

These verses remind us of the blessings, love, and provision that come from having a relationship with God and aligning our lives with His will.

Matthew 17:20

"Truly I tell you, if you have faith as small as a mustard seed, *you* can say to this mountain, 'Move from here to there,' and it will move. Nothing will be impossible for you." This verse highlights the power of faith and belief.

Matthew 17:20 is a statement made by Jesus to His disciples. In this verse, Jesus emphasizes the importance of having faith, even as small as a mustard seed. He tells His disciples that with such faith, they have the ability to command a mountain to move, and it will obey their command. This verse symbolizes the tremendous power of belief and trust in God's power to overcome seemingly insurmountable obstacles.

It is important to note that this verse is often interpreted metaphorically, rather than as a literal instruction to move physical mountains. It is seen as a call to have unwavering faith and to trust in God's power to accomplish great things in our lives.

Overall, this verse teaches the importance of having faith, even in the face of challenges, and the reminder that nothing is impossible for those who believe.

In a literal sense, if we were to dissect Matthew 17:20, it's important to acknowledge that Jesus used the concept of moving a mountain as an illustration to emphasize the power of faith and the ability to overcome obstacles.

If we were to apply it in a literal sense, it could suggest that with unwavering faith and belief, one could perform miracles and accomplish seemingly impossible feats, such as physically moving a mountain. However, it's crucial to note that this interpretation would be highly unconventional and not aligned with the general understanding of the verse and its intended metaphorical meaning.

The majority of biblical scholars and interpreters view this verse as metaphorical, highlighting the significance of faith rather than promoting a literal expectation of moving physical mountains. It is seen as a call to trust in God's power and believe in the possibility of overcoming challenges, no matter how daunting they may seem.

Taking a deeper analysis, this verse reminds believers of the limitless potential of faith. Just as a mustard seed is tiny but can grow into a large tree, our faith, no matter how small it may start, can become a powerful force in our lives. It encourages individuals to have unwavering trust in God, who can bring about miraculous transformations and provide solutions to seemingly impossible situations.

In summary, while a literal application of this verse would suggest the ability to physically move mountains, it is generally understood as a metaphorical expression of the power of faith and the capacity for overcoming obstacles through trust in God.

If a person applied this verse into their life, knowing that belief and faith will work according to their words, what type of life expectancy or quality of life would this person be living?

If a person genuinely applies the concept of Matthew 17:20 in their life, it can have a profound impact on their expectations and the quality of their life. Here's a breakdown of how this verse in action could influence an individual's life:

1. Increased confidence and optimism. Believing that their faith can move mountains; this person would develop an increased sense of confidence in their abilities. They would approach challenges with optimism, knowing that their faith can help overcome them.

2. Proactive problem-solving. With an unwavering belief in the power of faith, this person would be more inclined to actively seek solutions to problems instead of giving in to despair or hopelessness. They would have the confidence to think creatively and take action, knowing that their faith can bring about positive change.

3. Resilience in the face of adversity. A person applying Matthew 17:20 would understand that obstacles and setbacks are part of life. However, their faith would provide them with the strength and resilience to face adversity head-on, knowing that they have the power to overcome it.

4. Improved mental and emotional well-being. Belief in the power of faith can lead to a sense of peace and tranquility, reducing anxiety and stress. This person would have a more optimistic outlook on life, which can positively impact their mental and emotional well-being.

5. Greater purpose and fulfillment. Applying Matthew 17:20 can help this person cultivate a strong sense of purpose and fulfillment. They would have a deep understanding that their life has meaning and that they can make a difference by trusting in the power of their faith.

6. Positive impact on relationships. Believing that their faith can move mountains; this person would approach their relationships with love, compassion, and forgiveness. They would also see the potential for growth and transformation in themselves and others, fostering healthier and more fulfilling connections with those around them.

It's important to note that applying Matthew 17:20 does not mean that one will never face challenges or experience setbacks. However, it can significantly influence a person's mindset, attitudes, and actions, leading to a more positive and fulfilling life overall.

Matthew 17:20 broken down to a step-by-step process in a person's life.

1. Believe in the power of faith. Recognize and embrace the idea that faith has the potential to move mountains, metaphorically representing the obstacles and challenges we face in life.

2. Develop a strong conviction. Cultivate a deep and unwavering belief in the power of your faith. This conviction will serve as the foundation for taking action and expecting positive results.

3. Identify the mountain(s): Identify the specific challenges, obstacles, or goals that you want to address or achieve in your life. Clearly define what you want to overcome or accomplish.

4. Activate your faith: Take intentional steps to activate your faith through prayer, meditation, or other practices that strengthen your spiritual connection and belief system. Seek guidance, support, or inspiration from your chosen faith community.

5. Speak with authority: Use your words consciously and intentionally. Speak affirmations, declarations, or prayers that align with your faith and reinforce your belief that the mountains in your life can be moved or overcome. Avoid negative or self-defeating speech.

6. Align your actions: Ensure that your actions align with your faith and belief. Take positive steps towards your goals or in overcoming obstacles. Act with confidence, determination, and persistence, knowing that your faith supports your efforts.

7. Remain patient and persistent: Understand that moving mountains or achieving significant change may take time and effort. Stay patient and continue to hold onto your belief, even if results aren't immediate. Persevere and maintain your faith throughout the journey.

8. Celebrate progress and results. Recognize and celebrate the smaller victories and progress along the way. Acknowledge and give thanks for the positive changes that occur in your life as a result of applying your faith.

By understanding the process of faith growth using the analogy of a mustard seed, we can see that even the smallest seed of faith has the potential to grow into something significant. Matthew 17:20 encourages us to have the belief and trust that, with faith, we can move mountains and overcome the challenges that come our way in life.

Remember, this is a general step-by-step process, and the specifics may vary based on individual beliefs and interpretations. The key is to genuinely apply your faith, maintain a positive mindset, and take action aligned with your beliefs to see the transformational power of Matthew 17:20 in your life.

TESTIMONY
"I am what I am by choice or mistake."

Greeting Band of Brothers:

It is with great respect and admiration that I acknowledge the slogan you have chosen for yourself in your journey as a young Marine: "I am what I am by choice or mistake." These words resonate with a profound sense of individual agency and autonomy that underlines the strength of your character and the convictions you hold dear. Your choice of this slogan, stemming from your personal conflict and the resolution you found within yourself, reflects the unique and unwavering spirit that drives your decisions and actions.

Entering into the Marines during a time of war is a significant undertaking that demands courage, resilience, and a deep sense of commitment. It is a decision that carries immense weight and responsibility, requiring individuals to confront adversity, uphold honor, and stand ready to make sacrifices for the greater good. In the midst of such weighty considerations, it is no surprise that your process of decision-making was marked by moments of uncertainty and conflicting advice.

The conflict you experienced, wherein external voices urged caution and restraint while your heart called you to action, speaks volumes about the strength of your conviction and the clarity of your vision. It takes tremendous courage to navigate such discordant perspectives, especially when the stakes are so high. The fact that you chose to follow the stirrings of your heart and embrace the path that resonated most deeply within you is a testament to your unwavering resolve and sense of purpose.

Against the backdrop of uncertainty, the dedication and strength of character you have exhibited in making a decision, contrary to the advice of others, is truly remarkable. It takes a rare form of courage and self-assuredness to forge ahead on a path that diverges from the counsel of those around us. Your willingness to chart your own course in spite of conflicting guidance stands as a vivid testament to your tenacity and determination. It reflects a deep sense of self-awareness and an unyielding commitment to honor your own journey and integrity, even in the face of opposing counsel.

The slogan "I am what I am by choice or mistake" encapsulates the depth of your resolve and the unyielding spirit that has brought you to this pivotal moment in your life. It serves as a powerful reminder of your agency, your ability to make decisions and carve your own path, steering your destiny by your own deliberate choices. Embracing your identity and decisions as products of your own will demonstrates a profound sense of ownership and accountability that will undoubtedly serve as an anchor in the unpredictable waters of military service.

In choosing to heed the call within your heart and embrace the path that aligns with your deepest convictions, you embody a remarkable brand of resilience, integrity, and strength of character. Your decision serves as a testament to your unwavering dedication and unshakeable resolve, qualities that will undoubtedly serve you well as you navigate the challenges and triumphs that lie ahead.

As you move forward, know that your choices and sacrifices, born of your agency and firm resolve, will stand as a testament to the power of individual conviction and the indomitable spirit that resides within you. Your decision to remain true to yourself in the face of opposing advice is a testament to your unyielding dedication, and it is this dedication that will continue to guide and inspire you in your journey as a Marine.

Respectfully,
A fellow Marine

Aspiration
"I am what I am by choice or mistake."

- "I am what I am by choice," embracing my decisions with unwavering confidence and accountability, knowing that each choice shapes my unique journey.
- "I am what I am by mistake," recognizing that missteps and errors are integral to growth, and committing to learning from them with resilience and humility.
- I strive to embody the ethos of "I am what I am by

choice," embracing the power of deliberate decisions in shaping my character and destiny.
- Through the mantra of "I am what I am by mistake," I seek to forge a path of self-compassion, acknowledging that missteps are opportunities for introspection and refinement.
- Embracing the philosophy of "I am what I am by choice or mistake," I aspire to navigate life with a sense of agency and accountability, understanding that my actions shape my identity and impact on the world around me.

Affirmation
I am what I am by choice or mistake."

- I accept that "I am what I am by choice," and by mistake, understanding that both deliberate decisions and unintended errors contribute to my growth and character.
- I embrace the philosophy of "I am what I am by choice or mistake," acknowledging that my journey is shaped by both intentional actions and the lessons learned from missteps.
- I affirm my agency and accountability, owning the fact that "I am what I am by choice or mistake," and seeking to learn, grow, and evolve through both deliberate decisions and unforeseen errors.
- I honor the complexity of my journey, recognizing that "I am what I am by choice and mistake," weaving together the threads of my deliberate choices and the

invaluable lessons found in my missteps.

- I celebrate the totality of my experiences, understanding that "I am what I am by choice or mistake," and affirming my commitment to embrace the richness of both my conscious decisions and the wisdom gained from my inadvertent missteps.

Meaning

The phase "I am what I am by choice or mistake" encapsulates the idea that our identities and life paths are shaped not only by deliberate decisions but also by the unintended consequences of our actions. It acknowledges the complexity of human existence, encompassing both the intentional choices we make and the unforeseen errors or missteps we encounter along the way.

By stating, "I am what I am," the phrase emphasizes self-acceptance and self-awareness, acknowledging one's current state of being. The addition of "by choice or mistake" underscores the dual nature of human agency and fallibility. It highlights the role of conscious decision-making in shaping our lives, as well as the inevitable aspect of trial and error that accompanies the human experience.

Overall, the phrase "I am what I am by choice or mistake" carries a message of embracing one's authentic self, taking ownership of intentional decisions, and recognizing the transformative potential of learning from inadvertent missteps. It encourages individuals to embrace the entirety of their experiences, understanding that both volitional actions and unexpected outcomes contribute to the richness and depth of personal growth and self-discovery.

Bible verses

While the specific phrase "I am what I am by choice or mistake" is not found verbatim in the Bible, there are several verses that convey similar themes of personal responsibility, growth through mistakes, and the consequences of choices. Here are five Bible verses that relate to these concepts:

1. Proverbs 3:5-6 (NIV). "Trust in the Lord with all your heart and lean not on your own understanding; in all your ways submit to him, and he will make your paths straight." This verse emphasizes the importance of trusting in God's guidance and seeking wisdom in decision-making, acknowledging that our understanding may be limited.

2. Romans 8:28 (NIV). "And we know that in all things God works for the good of those who love him, who have been called according to His purpose." This verse highlights the belief that God can bring about positive outcomes even from our mistakes and challenges, reinforcing the idea of learning and growth through adversity.

3. Galatians 6:7 (NIV). "Do not be deceived: God cannot be mocked. A man reaps what he sows." This verse underscores the principle of personal accountability for our actions, emphasizing the idea that our choices have consequences, whether positive or negative.

4. Philippians 4:13 (NIV). "I can do all this through him who gives me strength." This verse speaks to the concept of drawing strength and resilience from a higher power, acknowledging that our personal abilities and limitations are intertwined with divine support.

5. 1 John 1:9 (NIV). "If we confess our sins, he is faithful and just and will forgive us our sins and purify us from all unrighteousness." This verse addresses the idea of seeking forgiveness and reconciliation after making mistakes, highlighting the opportunity for repentance and restoration in the face of errors.

While these verses may not directly contain the exact wording of "I am what I am by choice or mistake," they convey related concepts of decision-making, growth through challenges, personal responsibility, seeking divine guidance, and seeking forgiveness and restoration after making mistakes.

Your Purpose and Benefit

My dear believer in Christ,

I am delighted to respond to your inquiry about the significance of the "I am" statements of Jesus Christ and how they relate to your purpose and benefit as a follower of Christ. The "I am" statements attributed to Jesus carry profound meanings that provide insight into His divine mission and the blessings He offers to those who believe in Him. Let us explore these statements and their implications for your life as a believer.

1. "I am the bread of life" (John 6:35).

In referring to Himself as the "bread of life," Jesus emphasizes that He is the spiritual sustenance that nourishes and satisfies the deepest longings of the human soul. As a believer in Christ, your purpose within this "I am" statement is to partake of Jesus as the source of spiritual nourishment and to share this life-giving provision with others. You benefit from this by finding spiritual fulfillment and sustenance in Christ, enabling you to experience genuine satisfaction and purpose in your life.

2. "I am the light of the world" (John 8:12).

By proclaiming Himself as the "light of the world," Jesus reveals His role in dispelling spiritual darkness and illuminating the paths of those who follow him. As a believer, your purpose within this "I am" statement is to walk in the light of Christ and reflect His radiance to those around you. You benefit from this by receiving guidance, clarity, and understanding in your journey of faith, thereby avoiding stumbling in darkness and experiencing the freedom that comes from walking in the light of Christ.

3. "I am the door" (John 10:9).

Through the declaration of being the "door," Jesus illustrates that He is the gateway to a restored relationship with God and entry into the fullness of life. As a believer in Christ, your purpose within this "I am" statement is to embrace Jesus as the only access to the Father and to invite others to enter through this door of salvation. You benefit from this by finding security, protection, and access to an abundant life, rooted in the assurance of your eternal relationship with God.

4. "I am the good shepherd" (John 10:11).

In identifying Himself as the "good shepherd," Jesus portrays His role as the caring and sacrificial guardian of His flock. As a believer, your purpose within this "I am" statement is to trust in the loving care and guidance of Jesus, the Good Shepherd, and to extend that compassionate care to those in need. You benefit from this by experiencing the comforting presence, protection, and provision of Christ, who leads you to green pastures and still waters, nurturing your soul and offering you rest and restoration.

5. "I am the resurrection and the life" (John 11:25).

By declaring Himself as the "resurrection and the life," Jesus highlights His power over death and His ability to grant eternal life to all who believe in Him. Your purpose within this "I am" statement is to place your faith in Christ as the giver of eternal life and to share the hope of resurrection with others. You benefit from this by receiving the assurance of life beyond the grave, the comfort of knowing that death has been conquered, and the promise of eternal fellowship with God.

6. "I am the way, the truth, and the life" (John 14:6).

In proclaiming Himself as the "way, the truth, and the life," Jesus asserts His exclusive role as the path to God, the embodiment of truth, and the source of abundant life. As a believer, your purpose within this "I am" statement is to embrace Jesus as the sole mediator between God and humanity and to live out the truth of His teachings while sharing His offer of abundant life with others. You benefit from this by receiving the assurance of salvation, the revelation of divine truth, and the experience of abundant and fulfilling life in Christ.

7. "I am the true vine" (John 15:1).

By identifying Himself as the "true vine," Jesus symbolizes the essential connection between Himself and those who abide in Him, resulting in spiritual fruitfulness and growth. Your purpose within this "I am" statement is to remain in vital union with Christ, drawing nourishment from Him, and to bear the fruit of the Spirit, impacting the world for His glory. You benefit from this by experiencing spiritual vitality, productivity, and the fulfillment of your God-given potential as you abide in Christ, the true vine.

As a believer in Christ, your purpose within the "I am" statements of Jesus is to embrace Him as the fulfillment of your deepest needs, to proclaim His life-transforming message to others, and to reflect His character and teachings in your own life. Through this faithful alignment with the "I am" declarations, you benefit from the fullness of Christ's provision, guidance, and revelation, which empower you to live a life of purpose, hope, and eternal significance.

May you continue to seek, embrace, and testify to the profound truths encapsulated in the "I am" statements of Jesus Christ, finding your purpose and ultimate fulfillment in Him.

Yours in Christ,
Jesus

Chapter 5

༄༅

The Threefold Journey: Surrender, Transformation, and Responibility in Light of the Seven Identities of Jesus

Three stage process surrender, transformation, responsibility: The Concept of Surrendering to the Identity of Jesus

Transformation through Surrender to Christ: Unveiling the Essence of Being

Fulfilling the Covenant: Embracing Responsibility in Unity with the Creator

Take a marvelous journey with Jesus

As I walk

A lifetime Journey

Stage 1: Surrendering to Jesus Christ

Stage 2: Experiencing Transformation

Stage 3: Bearing Fruit and Sharing the Experience

Alignment with the Word of God

The journey of surrender, transformation, and responsibility in the context of our relationship with Jesus unfolds in a dynamic interplay with the seven identities of Christ, revealing deeper insights into our spiritual growth, identity, and mission as His followers. As we surrender our lives to Jesus, experience His transformative power, and embrace our responsibility in unity with Him, we mirror the essence of His divine nature and character through the lens of the seven "I am" statements, illuminating the profound and intimate connection between our journey and His identity.

Surrender marks the initial stage of our relationship with Jesus, as we yield our will, desires, and ambitions to His lordship and authority. Just as Jesus declared, "I am the way, the truth, and the life," our surrender to Him leads us on a path of truth, righteousness, and abundant life, as we acknowledge Him as the ultimate source of our salvation, guidance, and fulfillment. This act of surrender mirrors His identity as the embodiment of divine love, grace, and mercy, as we lay down our burdens and receive His yoke of rest and restoration.

Transformation emerges as the natural outgrowth of surrender, as we allow the power of Christ's love and presence to renew and reshape our hearts, minds, and spirits. Just as Jesus proclaimed, "I am the resurrection and the life," our transformation reflects His resurrection power at work within us, bringing dead places to life, healing brokenness, and restoring wholeness in every area of our being. This transformative process aligns us more closely with His identity as the source of eternal life, victory over sin and death, and abundant grace poured out for all who believe.

Responsibility emerges as the culmination of surrender and transformation, as we embrace our role as co-laborers with Christ in His redemptive mission and kingdom purposes. Just as Jesus declared, "I am the vine; you are the branches," our responsibility in unity with Him signifies our intimate connection and dependence on His life-giving presence and power, bearing fruit that testifies to His glory, love, and righteousness. This sense of responsibility mirrors His identity as the sustainer of all creation, the source of nourishment, strength, and vitality for His followers, who are called to abide in Him and bear witness to His transformative work in the world.

In essence, the three stages of surrender, transformation, and responsibility are intimately connected to the seven identities of Jesus, revealing the depth, richness, and significance of our relationship with Him as His beloved children and co-heirs of His kingdom. Through surrender, we acknowledge His lordship and authority over our lives, aligning ourselves with His truth, life, and way. Through transformation, we experience His power and presence at work within us, renewing and restoring us in His image and likeness. Through responsibility, we participate in His redemptive work, bearing fruit that reflects His character, mission, and love to a broken and hurting world.

May our journey of surrender, transformation, and responsibility be marked by humility, faithfulness, and obedience, as we seek to honor and glorify Jesus in all we do.

By embracing the essence of His seven identities, may we grow in grace, wisdom, and love, embodying the fullness of His divine nature and character in our lives and relationships, and shining brightly as beacons of hope, light, and truth in a world in need of His saving grace.

Three stage process surrender, transformation, responsibility: The Concept of Surrendering to the Identity of Jesus

Surrender is a fundamental aspect of the Christian faith, encapsulating the act of relinquishing one's will and desires to embrace the divine purpose and plan of God. In the context of the identities of Jesus, each aspect of His character and being beckons individuals to surrender their autonomy and submit to His sovereignty. One particular identity of Jesus that evokes a profound sense of surrender is His role as the Good Shepherd.

The imagery of Jesus as the Good Shepherd resonates deeply with the human soul, invoking feelings of protection, care, and guidance. The shepherd-sheep analogy conveys a sense of intimate relationship and dependency, where the sheep trust the shepherd for their well-being and sustenance. In embracing Jesus as the Good Shepherd, individuals are called to surrender their self-reliance and entrust their lives into His loving hands.

The concept of surrendering to Jesus as the Good Shepherd involves acknowledging our vulnerability and need for His provision and guidance. Just as sheep depend on their shepherd for protection and direction, we are invited to lay down our pride, fears, and anxieties at the feet of Jesus and allow Him to lead us on the path of righteousness. This act of surrender requires humility, faith, and a willingness to let go of control in order to follow the voice of the Shepherd.

Surrendering to Jesus as the Good Shepherd also means yielding to His authority and wisdom in our lives. As the ultimate Shepherd, Jesus knows each of His sheep intimately and is committed to leading them to green pastures and still waters. By surrendering our will to His divine leadership, we acknowledge His sovereignty and trust that His plans for us are good and purposeful. This surrender involves aligning our desires with His will, even when it may require sacrifice and stepping out in faith.

Furthermore, surrendering to Jesus as the Good Shepherd entails a deepening of our relationship with Him through intimacy and obedience. Just as sheep recognize the voice of their shepherd and follow him faithfully, we are called to cultivate a personal relationship with Jesus characterized by prayer, worship, and obedience to His teachings. This surrender is not a one-time event but a continuous journey of yielding our hearts and minds to the transformative work of the Holy Spirit.

In conclusion, the concept of surrendering to the identity of Jesus as the Good Shepherd encompasses an intimate, trusting, and obedient relationship with Him. Through surrender, we acknowledge His lordship over our lives, entrusting our fears and uncertainties into His capable hands. As we surrender our will to His divine guidance, we experience the peace, security, and abundance that come from following the Good Shepherd. May we echo the words of the psalmist, "The Lord is my shepherd; I lack nothing" (Psalm 23:1) and surrender wholeheartedly to His loving care and provision.

Philippians 2:9-11 (NIV) "Therefore God exalted him to the highest place and gave him the name that is above every name, that at the name of Jesus every knee should bow, in heaven and on earth and under the earth, and every tongue acknowledge that Jesus Christ is Lord, to the glory of God the Father."

Romans 10:9 (NIV) "That if you confess with your mouth, 'Jesus is Lord,' and believe in your heart that God raised him from the dead, you will be saved."

Transformation through Surrender to Christ: Unveiling the Essence of Being

Surrendering one's life to Christ as the Good Shepherd initiates a journey of transformation that transcends the surface level changes to the very essence of one's being. This process of transformation is multifaceted, encompassing spiritual, emotional, and relational dimensions that work together to unify the individual with the character and will of Christ. As we yield our will to the divine guidance of the Good Shepherd, we can expect several types of transformation that will mold us into His likeness.

At the core of transformation through surrender is the spiritual renewal that takes place within the surrendered soul. By surrendering our autonomy and submitting to Christ's lordship, we undergo a profound internal shift that redefines our identity and purpose. This spiritual transformation involves a deepening of faith, a restoration of hope, and reconciliation with God that brings about a new creation in Christ. Our hearts are regenerated, our minds renewed, and our spirits empowered by the indwelling presence of the Holy Spirit, leading us to walk in alignment with God's kingdom principles and values.

Emotionally, surrender to Christ as the Good Shepherd brings about a healing and restoration of the brokenness and wounds that have marred our lives. Through the process of surrender, we confront our fears, insecurities, and past hurts with the assurance of God's unconditional love and grace. As we lay down our burdens at the feet of Jesus, He carries our sorrows, comforts our hearts, and fills us with a supernatural peace that surpasses all understanding. This emotional transformation leads to a newfound resilience, joy, and freedom in Christ that enables us to face life's challenges with unwavering trust and confidence.

Moreover, surrendering to Christ as the Good Shepherd fosters relational transformation that deepens our connections with God and others. As we surrender our will to His divine plan, we are called to love sacrificially, forgive generously, and serve humbly in the footsteps of our Shepherd. This relational transformation extends to our interactions with family, friends, and even enemies, as we embody the love, compassion, and grace of Christ in our relationships. Through surrender, we become vessels of reconciliation, unity, and peace, reflecting the unity and harmony of the Trinity in our interactions with others.

Expectations of transformation through surrender to Christ also include a reorientation of our priorities, values, and ambitions in light of His kingdom purposes. As we align our will with His divine will, our desires are reshaped to prioritize the eternal over the temporal, the spiritual over the material, and the kingdom of God over the kingdom of self. This transformation involves a relinquishing of selfish ambitions, worldly pursuits, and sinful desires in exchange for a steadfast pursuit of righteousness, holiness, and obedience to God's will. Our lives become living testimonies of Christ's transformative power, drawing others to Him through our words and actions.

In essence, the transformation that occurs through surrender to Christ, as the Good Shepherd is a holistic process that redefines our identity, heals our wounds, deepens our relationships, and reorients our values toward His kingdom purposes. This transformation is not a one-time event but a lifelong journey of conformity to the image of Christ, as we continue to surrender our will, our hearts, and our lives to His loving care and guidance. May this transformation bring glory to God and bear witness to the transformative power of His redeeming love in our lives and in the world.

Romans 12:2 (NIV) "Do not conform to the pattern of this world but be transformed by the renewing of your mind. Then you will be able to test and approve what God's will is—His good, pleasing and perfect will."

Ezekiel 36:26 (NLT) "And I will give you a new heart, and I will put a new spirit in you. I will take out your stony, stubborn heart and give you a tender, responsive heart."

Fulfilling the Covenant: Embracing Responsibility in Unity with the Creator

As individuals who have surrendered their lives to Christ and experienced the transformative power of His love, we are called to embrace a profound sense of responsibility in our relationship with the Creator. This responsibility goes beyond mere obligations or duties; it reflects the covenantal bond that unites us with God in a sacred partnership of love, obedience, and unity. Just as the seven "I am" statements reveal the identity of Christ, our responsibility in this divine covenant is to embody the essence of being one with the Creator by aligning our hearts, minds, and actions with His will and character.

The concept of responsibility in unity with the Creator underscores our role as stewards of the relationship that God has initiated with us through Christ. This responsibility entails a deep commitment to walk in obedience, faithfulness, and intimacy with God, as we acknowledge Him as the ultimate source of our identity, purpose, and provision. Just as Jesus declared, "I am the vine; you are the branches," our responsibility is to abide in Him, drawing nourishment, strength, and vitality from our union with the true vine.

Furthermore, responsibility in unity with the Creator is rooted in the understanding that we are called to reflect the image and likeness of God in our lives, relationships, and spheres of influence. As Jesus proclaimed, "I am the light of the world," we are entrusted with the responsibility to shine the light of Christ brightly in a dark and broken world, illuminating the path of truth, love, and righteousness for others to see and follow. This responsibility calls us to embody the values, virtues, and virtues of Christ in all aspects of our lives, serving as ambassadors of His kingdom and bearers of His grace and mercy to those around us.

Moreover, responsibility in unity with the Creator involves the call to sacrificial love, service, and compassion towards others, mirroring the selfless nature of Christ's love for humanity. Just as Jesus declared, "I am the good shepherd," our responsibility is to emulate His example by caring for the spiritual, emotional, and physical needs of those entrusted to our care, guiding, protecting, and nurturing them with the same love and tenderness that our Shepherd lavishes upon us. This responsibility challenges us to prioritize the well-being and flourishing of others above our own interests, comforts, and ambitions, demonstrating the transformative power of Christ's love in action.

In essence, responsibility in unity with the Creator is an invitation to participate in the redemptive work of God's kingdom by embodying the values, virtues, and vocation of

Christ in our lives and relationships. This responsibility is not a burden to bear but a privilege to embrace, as we partner with God in fulfilling His purposes and advancing His kingdom on earth. As we align our will with His divine will, our hearts with His compassionate heart, and our actions with His righteous actions, we bear witness to the unity and harmony that exists between Creator and creation, reflecting the image and likeness of God in all we do.

May our responsibility in unity with the Creator be marked by humility, obedience, and love, as we seek to honor the covenantal relationship that binds us to God and to one another. Through our faithful stewardship of this sacred bond, may we bring glory to God, bear fruit that endures, and participate in the eternal work of redemption and reconciliation that Christ has inaugurated through His life, death, and resurrection.

2 Timothy 2:15 (KJV) "Study to shew thyself approved unto God, a workman that needeth not to be ashamed, rightly dividing the word of truth."

Ephesians 6:11 (ESV) "Put on the whole armor of God, that you may be able to stand against the schemes of the devil."

Take a marvelous journey with Jesus

It's great that you are seeking to establish a strong foundation in the Word of God and deepen your relationship with Him. Here are some key steps you can take to become a better steward towards God and honor Him in all areas of your life:

1. Daily Bible Study and Prayer. Set aside time each day to read and study the Bible. Pray for guidance, wisdom, and strength to live according to God's will.

2. Attend Church and Join a Bible Study Group. Regularly attend church services to worship with fellow believers and receive spiritual nourishment. Joining a Bible study group can help you grow in your understanding of God's Word and build relationships with other Christians.

3. Serve Others with Love. Look for opportunities to serve others in your community and church. Acts of kindness and service reflect the love of Christ and demonstrate your commitment to following His teachings.

4. Practice Generosity. Be generous with your resources, time, and talents. Giving back to God and others is a way to show gratitude for all that He has given you.

5. Seek God's Will in Decision-Making. Pray for discernment and seek God's guidance in all decisions you make, whether big or small. Trust His wisdom and direction to lead you on the right path.

6. Foster a Spirit of Gratitude. Cultivate a heart of thankfulness and praise towards God for His blessings and provisions in your life. A grateful heart leads to a deeper appreciation of God's goodness and faithfulness.

7. Repentance and Forgiveness. Regularly examine your heart and actions, confessing any sins or shortcomings to God. Seek His forgiveness and extend grace and forgiveness to others as well.

8. Live a Life of Integrity. Strive to live a life of honesty, integrity, and authenticity in all areas of your life. Let your words and actions reflect your commitment to following God's ways.

By actively engaging in these practices and seeking to align your life with the teachings of the Bible, you can cultivate a deeper relationship with God and become a faithful steward of His gifts and blessings. Remember, it is a journey of growth and transformation that requires perseverance, prayer, and reliance on God's grace.

This outline provides a structured overview of the key elements necessary for believers to be in right standing with God, emphasizing the foundational aspects of faith, the importance of relationship with God, living a transformed life, engaging in community and fellowship, practicing spiritual disciplines, and ultimately seeking to align one's life with God's will for His glory and our eternal fulfillment.

Studying and obeying God's Word is a foundational aspect of the Christian faith. The Scriptures emphasize the importance of immersing oneself in God's teachings, meditating on His precepts day and night, and aligning one's life with His commands. Through studying and obeying God's Word, believers cultivate a deeper understanding of His character, His will for their lives, and the path to true fulfillment and righteousness.

The concept of studying God's Word is not merely intellectual pursuit but a spiritual discipline that leads to transformation. In the Bible, God's Word is described as a lamp to our feet and a light to our path, guiding us through the complexities of life and illuminating the truth that sets us free. By diligently studying the Scriptures, believers gain wisdom, discernment, and insight into God's ways, enabling them to navigate challenges, make godly decisions, and grow in maturity and faith.

Moreover, obedience to God's Word is a natural outgrowth of genuine faith and reverence for God. Jesus Himself emphasized the importance of obedience, stating, "If you love me, keep my commands" (John 14:15). Obedience is not about legalistic adherence to rules but a heartfelt response of love and gratitude toward God for His grace and salvation. It is a surrender of one's will to God's divine authority, trusting in His wisdom and goodness above all else.

Through studying and obeying God's Word, believers experience transformation at the deepest levels of their being. The Word of God has the power to convict, challenge, comfort, and inspire, shaping their thoughts, attitudes, and actions according to God's perfect will. As they internalize the truths found in Scripture, believers are equipped to live out their faith in a world that often opposes God's ways, standing firm in their convictions and witnessing to the transformative power of Christ in their lives.

In essence, studying and obeying God's Word is a lifelong journey of growth and discovery, a pathway toward intimacy with God and conformity to Christ's likeness. It requires discipline, humility, and a reliance on the Holy Spirit to illuminate the Scriptures and guide believers into all truth. As they study God's Word with a teachable heart and obey its principles with faith-filled obedience, believers are transformed from the inside out, becoming vessels of God's love, light, and grace in a world desperately in need of His truth and redemption.

As I walk

In walking with Christ, it's essential to remember that these responsibilities are not burdensome tasks but joyful opportunities to grow closer to God and be a light to the world. By studying and obeying God's Word, seeking truth, walking by faith, trusting in God's grace, and giving thanks in all circumstances, you align your life with His will and experience the fullness of His blessings.

Remember to approach your responsibilities with a humble and grateful heart, knowing that it is by God's grace and mercy that you are able to fulfill them. Stay connected to Him through prayer, fellowship with other believers, and by sharing His love and encouragement with those around you. As you continue to seek and follow God's ways, may your faith deepen, your joy increase, and your life reflect the transformative power of Christ within you.

In the process of surrendering to the Lord and experiencing a transformation from being a child of wrath to a child of faith, the "I am the light of the world" statement by Jesus in John 8:12 would be particularly significant. This statement emphasizes the transition from walking in darkness to walking in the light, symbolizing the profound change and renewal that occurs when one commits their life to following Jesus. As individuals embrace Jesus as the light of the world, they are guided, illuminated, and transformed in their journey of faith, leaving behind the darkness of their past and stepping into a new life filled with His light, truth, and grace.

The "I am" statements of Jesus in the Gospel of John reveal different aspects of His identity and purpose. For someone going through the process of surrendering their life to the Lord, the following three statements may be particularly impactful:

1. "I am the way, the truth, and the life" (John 14:6). This statement highlights that Jesus is not just a way to salvation; He is the only way. Surrendering one's life to the Lord involves acknowledging Jesus as the sole path to God, truth, and eternal life. Embracing Jesus as the ultimate Truth and Life can provide comfort and guidance to those navigating the journey of surrender.

2. "I am the vine; you are the branches" (John 15:5). This metaphor emphasizes the intimate relationship between Jesus and His followers. Surrendering to the Lord involves abiding in Him, drawing nourishment and strength from Him. Just as branches derive their life from the vine, surrendering to Jesus involves complete reliance on Him for spiritual sustenance and growth.

3. "I am the resurrection and the life" (John 11:25).

This statement reassures believers that Jesus has power over death and offers eternal life to those who believe in Him. Surrendering one's life to the Lord involves embracing the hope of resurrection and the promise of eternal life through Jesus. This reassurance can bring comfort and courage to those facing the unknowns of surrender and transformation.

These "I am" statements encapsulate essential truths about Jesus that can guide and strengthen individuals as they surrender their lives to Him. By emphasizing Jesus as the exclusive path to God, highlighting the intimate connection between Him and believers, and offering the assurance of eternal life, these statements can provide comfort, direction, and purpose to those in the process of surrendering their lives to the Lord.

A lifetime Journey

These Bible verses underscore the importance of surrendering ourselves to Christ, shifting from self-centeredness to a God-centered focus, and living in alignment with His will and purposes.

The perspective on the seven "I am" statements of Jesus and the three-stage process I have outlined is a beautiful way to explore the transformative power of faith in one's life. Let's break it down into three stages and explore how each of these stages can impact individuals.

Stage 1: Surrendering to Jesus Christ

In this stage, surrendering one's life and will unto Jesus Christ is the first step towards a transformative journey. This act of surrendering involves letting go of one's own desires and submitting to the will of God. It signifies a shift in focus from self-centeredness to God-centeredness, allowing for a profound change to take place within the individual. This surrendering opens the door for a personal encounter with Jesus, leading to a deep transformation in various aspects of life.

Stage 2: Experiencing Transformation

Once the surrender has taken place, the individual embarks on a journey of personal growth and transformation. This stage involves a significant change in one's character, attitudes, and behavior. It's akin to a spiritual makeover where the individual is increasingly molded into the likeness of Christ. The transformation experienced in this stage is not merely external but also internal, affecting one's thoughts, emotions, and relationships. This process of renewal is a continual journey of growth in faith and understanding of God's will.

Stage 3: Bearing Fruit and Sharing the Experience

In the final stage, the transformed individual becomes a bearer of the fruit of their faith. This involves living out the values and teachings of Jesus in daily life and sharing the experience of transformation with others. As a reflection of God's love and grace, the individual becomes an instrument of spreading the light of Christ to those around them. By sharing their testimony and proclaiming the goodness of God, they invite others to experience the same transformative power in their own lives. This stage emphasizes the responsibility of believers to be witnesses of God's love and grace in the world.

Alignment with the Word of God

Your three-stage process aligns well with the fundamental teachings of Christianity, emphasizing themes of surrender, transformation, and sharing the gospel. The "I am" statements of Jesus, such as "I am the way, the truth, and the life" (John 14:6) and "I am the vine; you are the branches" (John 15:5), provide a rich foundation for understanding the transformative power of faith in Christ. These statements highlight the identity of Jesus as the source of life and the pathway to salvation.

Conclusion

In summary, the three-stage process offers a powerful framework for understanding the impact of the "I am" statements of Jesus on the lives of individuals. By surrendering to Christ, experiencing transformation, and bearing fruit in sharing the gospel, believers embody the core principles of Christian faith. This cyclical process of surrender, transformation, and witness reflects the ongoing journey of growth and discipleship in the Christian walk. Through embracing these stages, individuals can deepen their relationship with God and have a profound impact on the lives of others.

Psalms 23 (NIV). The Lord is my shepherd, I lack nothing. He makes me lie down in green pastures; he leads me beside quiet waters, he refreshes my soul. He guides me along the right paths for His name's sake. Even though I walk through the darkest valley, I will fear no evil, for you are with me; Your rod and your staff, they comfort me. You prepare a table before me in the presence of my enemies. You anoint my head with oil; my cup overflows. Surely your goodness and love will follow me all the days of my life, and I will dwell in the house of the Lord forever.

Chapter 6

ॐ

THE FOUR PHASES OF WHO AM I

Phase 1. Personal Authenticity: Embracing Your True Self

Phase 2. External Perceptions: The Mirror of Society

How to balance seeking validation from others and staying true to yourself.

How to establish boundaries with people who are constantly seeking your validation.

The importance of self-validation versus external validation: The foundation of self-worth and personal growth.

Phase 3. Divine Perspective: A Higher Gaze

When God calls my name

Phase 4. Profound nature of Jesus' identity and mission

Matthew 16:13-17

"When Jesus came to the region of Caesarea Philippi, he asked His disciples, 'Who do people say the Son of Man is?' They replied, 'Some say John the Baptist; others say Elijah; and still others, Jeremiah or one of the prophets.' 'But what about you?' he asked. 'Who do you say I am?' Simon Peter answered, 'You are the Messiah, the Son of the living God.' Jesus replied, 'Blessed are you, Simon son of Jonah, for this was not revealed to you by flesh and blood, but by my Father in heaven.'"

This interaction between Jesus and His disciples showcases a significant moment where Jesus, identifying as the Son of Man, firmly embodies His authentic human experience and His mission to bring salvation and redemption to all.

Based on the conversation that Jesus had with His disciples I would like to break it down into three different aspects of a person's identity.

- First, inspect how do I view myself, my personal authenticity.
- Second, how do people view me?
- Third, how does God view me?

This breakdown of the conversation into three aspects of a person's identity – how one views oneself (personal authenticity), how others view them, and how God views them – is a thoughtful way to interpret the interaction between Jesus and His disciples regarding identity. Let's explore each aspect further based on the context of the conversation:

1. Personal Authenticity - "Who do I view myself as?"

In the conversation, Jesus first asks His disciples who people say He is, prompting them to consider the perceptions others have of Him. This question can also be applied introspectively to oneself. It encourages reflection on how individuals perceive their own identities, beliefs, values, and purpose. Understanding and embracing one's personal authenticity involves self-awareness, self-acceptance, and alignment with one's true values and beliefs.

2. How Others View Me - "Who do people view me as?"

The disciples respond to Jesus by sharing the various opinions people have about him – some see Him as John the Baptist, Elijah, Jeremiah, or one of the prophets. This aspect pertains to external perception and societal influence on an individual's identity. People's opinions, expectations, and judgments can shape how one is perceived in the world. It highlights the importance of self-reflection, understanding how others perceive you, and discerning which external influences align with your personal authenticity.

3. How God Views Me - "How does God view me?"

When Jesus specifically asks His disciples, "But what about you? Who do you say I am? He is directing their focus to their personal beliefs and convictions about His identity. Peter's response, acknowledging Jesus as the Messiah, the Son of the living God, signifies a profound faith-based perspective that goes beyond human perceptions. Applying this to personal identity, considering how God views an individual involves spiritual or transcendent aspects of identity. It encompasses faith, purpose, divine calling, and one's relationship with the divine.

Overall, the breakdown proposed provides a structured framework for examining different dimensions of identity - internal self-perception, external societal perceptions, and transcendent or spiritual perspectives. It encourages individuals to reflect on their self-image, societal influences, and spiritual beliefs to cultivate a deeper understanding of their identity and purpose. This approach can lead to greater self-awareness, authenticity, and alignment with one's values and beliefs.

Phase 1
Personal Authenticity: Embracing Your True Self

In this phase, we delve into the concept of personal authenticity – the core of who you are. Through introspection and self-reflection, we explore how you view yourself, your values, beliefs, and unique qualities. Discovering and accepting your authentic self allows you to align with your true identity, leading to a deeper sense of self-awareness and fulfillment.

Personal authenticity is the foundation upon which we build our identities and navigate our lives. It is the essence of embracing our true selves, acknowledging our core values, beliefs, and unique qualities that define who we are at our very core. At the heart of personal authenticity lies the concept of purpose - the driving force that gives meaning and direction to our existence.

Purpose is not merely a goal to achieve or a destination to reach; it is the deep-seated understanding of why we are here, what we are meant to do, and how we can make a meaningful contribution to the world around us. When we embrace our personal authenticity, we are aligning ourselves with our true selves, leading to a profound sense of purpose that guides our actions and decisions.

The fulfillment of personal authenticity goes beyond surface-level expressions of identity; it is about living in accordance with our deepest values and beliefs, honoring our inner truths, and staying true to who we are at our core. This authenticity allows us to navigate the complexities of life with clarity, integrity, and resilience, paving the way for a sense of fulfillment that comes from living a life that is true to ourselves.

Acknowledging our true selves requires courage, vulnerability, and a willingness to explore our innermost thoughts and emotions. It involves peeling back the layers of societal expectations, external influences, and self-imposed limitations to reveal the authentic self that lies beneath. By embracing our true selves, we cultivate a sense of self-awareness and self-acceptance that forms the bedrock of personal authenticity.

The journey of personal authenticity is not always easy; it may involve confronting fears, breaking free from ingrained patterns of behavior, and challenging the status quo. However, the rewards of this journey are immeasurable - a deep sense of inner peace, a profound connection to our true purpose, and a heightened awareness of the unique gifts and talents we bring to the world.

In essence, personal authenticity is about living a life that is true to ourselves, honoring our values, beliefs, and inner truths, and embracing the fullness of who we are. It is a journey of self-discovery, growth, and transformation that leads to a profound sense of fulfillment and purpose. When we acknowledge our true selves and live authentically, we not only benefit ourselves but also contribute positively to the world around us, inspiring others to do the same.

Embracing our personal authenticity and acknowledging our true selves is a powerful act of self-love and self-empowerment. It is a gift we give ourselves and the world, a testament to our inner strength, resilience, and capacity for growth. By living authentically and honoring the essence of who we are, we not only find fulfillment and purpose but also inspire others to do the same, creating a ripple effect of authenticity, compassion, and positive change in the world.

Embracing personal authenticity in daily life involves aligning our actions, decisions, and interactions with our true selves, honoring our values, beliefs, and unique qualities. Here are some examples of how we can cultivate personal authenticity in various aspects of our lives:

1. In Relationships. Being authentic in relationships means communicating openly and honestly, expressing your true thoughts and feelings without fear of judgment or rejection. This can lead to deeper connections with others based on trust, understanding, and mutual respect. For example, if you have a disagreement with a friend or loved one, you can approach the conversation with authenticity by expressing your viewpoint respectfully and listening openly to their perspective.

2. At Work. Embracing personal authenticity in the workplace involves staying true to your values and principles, even in challenging situations. It means being transparent about your strengths and weaknesses, advocating for your ideas and opinions, and standing up for what you believe in. For instance, if you feel that a project at work goes against your values, you can speak up and offer constructive feedback in a respectful and professional manner.

3. Self-Expression. Personal authenticity can be expressed through creative outlets such as art, music, writing, or any form of self-expression that resonates with you. Embrace your unique voice, style, and perspective without comparison or self-censorship. Whether it's writing poetry that reflects your inner thoughts and emotions or creating art that expresses your vision of the world, allow yourself to be fully authentic in your creative endeavors.

4. Making Choices. Authentic living involves making choices that are true to your desires, passions, and aspirations. When faced with decisions, consider whether each option aligns with your values and long-term goals. For example, if you are contemplating a career change, reflect on whether the new path resonates with your authentic self and brings you closer to living a life that is meaningful and fulfilling.

5. Mindfulness and Self-Care. Practicing mindfulness and self-care are essential components of embracing personal authenticity. Take time to connect with yourself, listen to your inner voice, and prioritize activities that nourish your mind, body, and spirit. Whether it's through meditation, journaling, nature walks, or other forms of self-reflection, create space for self-discovery and self-compassion in your daily routine.

6. Setting Boundaries. Honoring your personal boundaries is a key aspect of living authentically. Learn to assert your needs and limits in relationships, work situations, and other areas of your life. By setting healthy boundaries, you protect your well-being, uphold your values, and create space for authentic connections with others based on mutual respect and understanding.

7. Authenticity in Communication. Communicate authentically by speaking your truth with clarity, empathy, and integrity. Express yourself in a way that is genuine and respectful, whether you are sharing your opinions, emotions, or experiences. Practice active listening and strive to understand others' perspectives with an open mind and heart.

By incorporating these examples of embracing personal authenticity into your daily life, you can cultivate a deeper sense of self-awareness, empowerment, and fulfillment. Remember that authenticity is a journey of self-discovery and growth, and each step you take towards embracing your true self brings you closer to living a life that is aligned with your values, purpose, and essence.

Phase 2
External Perceptions: The Mirror of Society

This phase focuses on how others perceive you and the impact of societal influences on your identity. Just as the disciples shared different opinions about Jesus' identity, external perceptions can shape how others see you. Understanding the role of societal expectations, judgments, and influences reveals the importance of discerning which external factors align with your true self, and which ones may require reflection or adjustment.

In a world where social interactions and relationships play a significant role in shaping our identities and experiences, external perception serves as a mirror reflecting how we are viewed by others in society. While this reflection can provide valuable insights into our impact on the world around us, it also raises questions about the balance between seeking validation from others and staying true to our authentic selves.

External perception acts as a lens through which we view ourselves in relation to others. It encompasses the way we are perceived based on our actions, words, appearance, and interactions with the world. This perception can influence our self-esteem, sense of belonging, and social standing, shaping our understanding of how we fit into the fabric of society.

The purpose of external perception lies in its ability to offer feedback on our behavior, attitudes, and values, providing an external perspective that can help us grow, adapt, and navigate social dynamics. By considering how others perceive us, we gain valuable insights into our impact on the world and opportunities for self-improvement and personal growth.

The meaning of external perception extends beyond mere judgments or opinions from others. It can reflect societal norms, expectations, biases, and cultural values that shape our interactions and relationships. By understanding how we are perceived in different social contexts, we gain a deeper insight into the complexities of human connection and the power dynamics at play in our interactions with others.

Our passion for acceptance, recognition, and belonging can drive us to seek validation from external sources, including friends, family, colleagues, and society at large. This desire for approval is rooted in our innate need for connection and affirmation, fueling our efforts to present ourselves in ways that align with social norms and expectations.

While valuing external perception can offer benefits in terms of social integration, feedback, and growth, it also raises questions about the potential pitfalls of placing too much emphasis on how others see us. When we prioritize external validation over our own values, beliefs, and authenticity, we risk losing sight of our true selves in the pursuit of approval and acceptance.

Valuing external perception can provide valuable feedback, insights, and opportunities for self-improvement and growth. By considering how others perceive us, we can gain a more nuanced understanding of our impact on the world, enhance our communication skills, and build stronger relationships based on empathy, respect, and understanding.

Valuing external perception to the point of losing your own self-worth. This is placing excessive value on external perception, which can lead to a phenomenon known as "people-pleasing," where individuals prioritize others' opinions and expectations over their own well-being and authenticity. This can result in feelings of insecurity, anxiety, and disconnection from one's true self, as the constant quest for approval and validation erodes self-worth and undermines personal integrity.

The pressure to meet societal standards, fit in, and gain approval can become overwhelming, leading to feelings of stress, inadequacy, and self-doubt. When we prioritize external perception at the expense of our own values, passions, and well-being, we risk sacrificing our authenticity and sense of self-worth in a futile attempt to please others and conform to external expectations.

In conclusion, while external perception can offer valuable insights and feedback, it is essential to strike a balance between seeking validation from others and staying true to our authentic selves. By valuing our own self-worth, beliefs, and values, we can navigate social dynamics with confidence, integrity, and authenticity, creating meaningful connections and relationships based on mutual respect and understanding. Embracing our true selves and honoring our authenticity is the key to living a fulfilling and purposeful life, free from the constraints of external judgments and expectations.

How to balance seeking validation from others and staying true to yourself.

Balancing seeking validation from others and staying true to yourself is a delicate dance that requires self-awareness, confidence, and a strong sense of personal identity. Here are some tips to help you navigate this balance:

1. Self-Reflection. Take time to reflect on your values, beliefs, and passions. Understand what is truly important to you and what defines your sense of self. This self-awareness will serve as a compass to guide your decisions and actions.

2. Set Boundaries. Establish clear boundaries around what feedback and opinions you value from others. Be selective in whose opinions you seek and consider, choosing those who genuinely care about your well-being and growth.

3. Seek Feedback Wisely. Rather than seeking validation for validation's sake, seek constructive feedback that can help you grow and improve. Be open to different perspectives but filter them through your own values and priorities.

4. Practice Self-Validation. Develop a practice of self-compassion and self-affirmation. Acknowledge your achievements, strengths, and uniqueness without needing external validation to feel worthy or validated.

5. Trust Your Intuition. Listen to your inner voice and trust your instincts. Pay attention to how certain situations, people, or choices make you feel, and use that information to make decisions that align with your authentic self.

6. Surround Yourself with Supportive People. Cultivate relationships with individuals who accept you for who you are, support your growth, and encourage you to be true to yourself. Surrounding yourself with positive influences can reinforce your sense of self-worth and authenticity.

7. Practice Assertiveness. Communicate your boundaries, values, and needs assertively with others. Be clear about what is important to you and advocate for yourself in a respectful and confident manner.

8. Focus on Personal Growth. Shift your focus from seeking external validation to prioritizing personal growth and self-improvement. Set goals that align with your values and work towards realizing your full potential, independent of others' judgments or opinions.

9. Embrace Imperfection. Understand that seeking perfection or approval from others is an unattainable goal. Embrace your imperfections, mistakes, and vulnerabilities as part of what makes you uniquely human and worthy of self-compassion.

10. Practice Mindfulness. Stay present in the moment and cultivate mindfulness practices that help you tune into your thoughts, emotions, and reactions. Mindfulness can help you stay grounded in your authentic self and resist the pressures of seeking external validation.

By integrating these strategies into your daily life, you can cultivate a healthy balance between seeking validation from others and staying true to yourself. Remember that your worth and identity are not defined by external perceptions or opinions but by your own self-awareness, values, and authenticity. Trust in your inner wisdom and embrace the journey of self-discovery and growth with confidence and resilience.

Balancing the act of seeking validation from others while staying true to oneself is a delicate dance that demands self-awareness, confidence, and a deepening sense of personal identity. It is a tightrope walk between the external world's perceptions and the internal compass of one's authentic self. This concept is not merely a matter of balancing conflicting desires; it is a dynamic process that evolves with personal growth and introspection.

Seeking validation from others is a fundamental aspect of human nature. We inherently crave recognition, acceptance, and affirmation from our external environment. It can provide valuable feedback, guidance, and a sense of belonging. However, relying too heavily on external validation can lead to a loss of autonomy and authenticity. When our sense of self-worth hinges on the approval of others, we risk compromising our values, beliefs, and aspirations in pursuit of external validation.

On the other hand, staying true to oneself requires a deep understanding of one's core values, beliefs, and aspirations. It involves listening to the inner voice that guides us towards our true purpose and passions. Being true to oneself means honoring personal values, nurturing self-respect, and embracing individuality without being swayed by external influences. It is a journey of self-discovery and self-acceptance that requires courage, vulnerability, and a commitment to authenticity.

The key to balancing seeking validation from others and staying true to oneself lies in cultivating self-awareness. Self-awareness allows us to discern between constructive feedback and external expectations that do not align with our authentic self. By developing a keen understanding of our strengths, weaknesses, and motivations, we can navigate the complex interplay between external validation and internal truth.

Confidence plays a vital role in this balancing act. A strong sense of self-confidence empowers us to trust our instincts, stand firm in our convictions, and resist the pressure to conform to external standards. True confidence stems from self-acceptance and self-love, enabling us to embrace our uniqueness and express our genuine selves authentically.

Furthermore, maintaining a growing sense of personal identity is essential in striking a harmonious balance between seeking validation from others and staying true to oneself. Personal identity evolves over time through experiences, reflections, and self-exploration. As we deepen our understanding of who we are and what we stand for, we become less reliant on external validation to define our worth and significance.

In conclusion, the concept of balancing seeking validation from others and staying true to oneself is a nuanced journey of self-discovery, self-acceptance, and self-expression. It requires a delicate dance that unfolds through self-awareness, confidence, and a steadfast connection to one's evolving personal identity. By navigating this intricate balance with mindfulness and authenticity, we can cultivate a sense of inner harmony, fulfillment, and empowerment that transcends the ebb and flow of external validation.

How to establish boundaries with people who are constantly seeking your validation.

Establishing boundaries with people who constantly seek your validation can be challenging but essential for maintaining your own sense of self-worth and autonomy. Here are some steps you can take to set healthy boundaries in these situations:

1. Identify Your Limits. Recognize when someone's constant need for validation is draining your energy, impacting your well-being, or compromising your own values and priorities. Understanding your limits will help you determine where to set boundaries effectively.

2. Communicate Clearly. Express your thoughts and feelings honestly and assertively to the person seeking validation. Let them know that while you value their opinions, you also need space to focus on your own growth and priorities. Be direct but compassionate in your communication.

3. Set Limits on Your Availability. Establish clear boundaries around your availability to provide validation. Let the person know when and how you are willing to offer support or feedback and communicate when you need time for yourself or other commitments.

4. Redirect Their Focus. Encourage the person to explore their own self-worth and strengths independently. Redirect their focus towards developing self-validation strategies and building confidence in their own abilities without relying solely on external feedback.

5. Encourage Independence. Empower the individual to make decisions and take actions autonomously.

Encourage them to trust their own judgment, seek self-improvement, and cultivate self-awareness without constantly seeking validation from others.

6. Model Healthy Behavior. Lead by example by demonstrating self-validation and self-reliance in your own life. Show the person that it is possible to feel confident and secure in oneself without constantly seeking external validation.

7. Practice Empathy. Understand that the person's constant need for validation may stem from deeper insecurities or self-doubt. Approach the situation with empathy and compassion, while still maintaining your own boundaries and self-care.

8. Limit Exposure. If the person's behavior continues to be emotionally draining or overwhelming, consider limiting your exposure to them. Create physical, emotional, or time boundaries to protect your own well-being and reduce the impact of their constant validation-seeking behavior on you.

9. Seek Support. If you are struggling to set boundaries with someone who constantly seeks your validation, seek support from friends, family, or a therapist. Discuss your concerns, receive feedback, and explore strategies for maintaining healthy boundaries in the relationship.

10. Reinforce Positive Behavior. Acknowledge and reinforce instances where the person demonstrates self-validation and self-confidence. Celebrate their growth and progress towards developing a healthier relationship with themselves, reinforcing positive behavior patterns.

Remember that establishing boundaries is a form of self-care and self-respect. It is important to prioritize your own well-being and values while navigating relationships with others. By communicating assertively, setting limits, and encouraging self-reliance in those seeking constant validation, you can create healthier dynamics that support mutual growth and respect.

Establishing boundaries with people who are constantly seeking your validation can be a challenging yet essential aspect of maintaining your own sense of self-worth and autonomy. It requires a deep understanding of your own values, assertiveness in asserting your boundaries, and a commitment to prioritizing your well-being above the need to please others. This dynamic process can be both empowering and liberating as you take control of your own validation and assert your right to authenticity and self-respect.

When dealing with individuals who constantly seek your validation, it can feel overwhelming and draining. Their incessant need for approval and reassurance can blur the lines between your own needs and theirs, leading to a loss of personal boundaries and a sense of being emotionally consumed. It is crucial to recognize that your worth does not depend on meeting the expectations of others or constantly seeking their approval. Your self-worth is inherent and should not be diminished by the validation of others.

Establishing boundaries with these individuals is a fundamental step in reclaiming your autonomy and preserving your emotional well-being. Boundaries serve as a protective shield that delineates where you end and others begin, guiding how you interact with those who seek your validation. Setting boundaries involves clearly communicating your limits, expectations, and needs while respecting those of others. It is about asserting your values, desires, and priorities without compromising your integrity or sacrificing your emotional health.

Assertiveness plays a crucial role in establishing and maintaining boundaries with people who constantly seek your validation. It entails expressing your thoughts, feelings, and boundaries in a clear and direct manner while respecting the perspectives of others. By practicing assertiveness, you can communicate your needs assertively and advocate for your well-being without resorting to passive or aggressive behavior. Assertiveness empowers you to set boundaries firmly and assert your right to self-respect and authenticity.

Moreover, prioritizing your well-being above the need to please others is essential in navigating relationships with individuals who constantly seek your validation. It involves honoring your own needs, values, and emotions instead of sacrificing them to fulfill the expectations of others. Prioritizing self-care and self-respect allows you to establish boundaries that protect your mental and emotional space, leading to healthier, more fulfilling relationships based on mutual respect and understanding.

In the process of setting boundaries with individuals who seek your validation, it is important to remember that self-worth comes from within. Your value is not determined by how others perceive or validate you, but by how you perceive and validate yourself. By affirming your worth, embracing your uniqueness, and honoring your authenticity, you can cultivate a strong sense of self-worth that is not contingent on external validation.

In conclusion, establishing boundaries with people who constantly seek your validation is a vital component of maintaining your self-worth and autonomy. It requires self-awareness, assertiveness, and a commitment to prioritizing your well-being above the need to please others. By setting clear boundaries, practicing assertiveness, and prioritizing self-care, you can navigate relationships with confidence, integrity, and authenticity. Remember that your worth is inherent and does not rely on external validation. Embrace your uniqueness, honor your boundaries, and assert your right to self-respect and autonomy.

The importance of self-validation versus external validation: The foundation of self-worth and personal growth

In conclusion, the essence of self-validation versus external validation is crucial. While it's natural to compare and compete, the focus should always remain on yourself. Your dreams and aspirations should spring from your own passion, not influenced by others. Don't let anyone hinder or spur your personal growth. Ultimately, ambition should come from within, driving you towards fulfilling your potential without relying on external validation. Stay true to your path and continue striving for greater heights that align with your inner aspirations and values.

The importance of self-validation versus external validation lies in the foundation of self-worth and personal growth. While external validation can provide temporary boosts to our self-esteem, true fulfillment and confidence come from within. Here are key points to consider:

Self-validation is crucial because:
1. **Authenticity.** When we validate ourselves, we align our actions and decisions with our true values and beliefs, leading to a more authentic and fulfilling life.

2. **Independence.** Relying on external validation makes us dependent on others for self-worth, while self-validation fosters independence and self-reliance.

3. **Resilience.** Self-validation builds resilience and inner strength, enabling us to navigate challenges and setbacks with confidence and self-assurance.

4. **Self-Discovery.** By validating ourselves, we embark on a journey of self-discovery, understanding our strengths, weaknesses, and passions on a deeper level.

5. **Empowerment.** Self-validation empowers us to pursue our dreams and aspirations wholeheartedly, without seeking constant approval from others.

While it's natural to compare ourselves to others and seek inspiration from external sources, the essence of growth lies in competing with oneself for continuous improvement and self-empowerment. Here's why it's essential to focus on self-comparison and self-competition:

1. Personal Growth. Comparing yourself to your past self allows for personal growth and progress, as you strive to be better than you were yesterday.

2. Intrinsic Motivation. Competing with yourself cultivates intrinsic motivation driven by your own goals and aspirations, rather than external pressures or influences.

3. Self-Reflection. Self-comparison promotes self-reflection and introspection, enabling you to identify areas for improvement and set meaningful goals based on your own values and desires.

4. Empowerment. Being in competition with yourself fosters a sense of empowerment and ownership over your life journey, leading to greater fulfillment and satisfaction.

5. Uniqueness. Recognizing that your journey is unique and incomparable to others allows you to embrace your individuality and pursue your dreams without being swayed by external expectations or judgments.

Ultimately, your dreams and aspirations should be fueled by the passion in your heart, guided by your inner compass, and driven by a deep sense of purpose and fulfillment. Do not let others' opinions or actions hinder your path to success or diminish your worth and ambitions. Stay focused on your personal growth, celebrate your progress, and continue striving towards realizing your life dreams with unwavering determination and self-belief. You are the architect of your own destiny, and no one should stand in the way of your journey towards personal wealth, worth, and ambition.

The importance of self-validation versus external validation is deeply rooted in the foundation of self-worth and personal growth. While external validation can provide temporary boosts to our self-esteem, true fulfillment and confidence come from within. Understanding this distinction is crucial in cultivating a strong sense of self-worth, fostering personal development, and nurturing a healthy relationship with oneself and others.

External validation, in the form of praise, approval, or acceptance from others, can be alluring and gratifying. It often serves as a quick fix for boosting our self-esteem and reinforcing our sense of worth. However, relying solely on external validation can be a precarious foundation for our self-worth. It places our sense of worthiness in the hands of others, making us vulnerable to fluctuations in their opinions, judgments, and expectations. Seeking validation from external sources can lead to a cycle of seeking approval, comparison, and validation-seeking behaviors that undermine our autonomy and hinder our personal growth.

On the other hand, self-validation is the process of acknowledging, accepting, and affirming our own thoughts, feelings, and experiences without seeking approval or validation from others. It involves recognizing our intrinsic value, honoring our emotions, and validating our own worthiness independent of external factors. Self-validation is an inner compass that guides us in affirming our authenticity, acknowledging our strengths and limitations, and nurturing a deep sense of self-acceptance and self-respect.

The foundation of self-worth lies in our ability to validate ourselves from within. When we recognize and affirm our worth independently of external validation, we cultivate a resilient sense of self-esteem that is not contingent on the opinions or actions of others. Self-validation empowers us to embrace our uniqueness, celebrate our achievements, and navigate challenges with confidence and self-assurance. It allows us to define our worth on our own terms, based on our values, beliefs, and principles, rather than seeking validation from external sources.

Moreover, self-validation is essential for personal growth and development. It serves as a catalyst for introspection, self-awareness, and self-improvement. By validating our own experiences, emotions, and decisions, we gain insight into our strengths, vulnerabilities, and areas for growth. Self-validation encourages self-reflection, self-compassion, and self-empowerment, nurturing a positive self-image and fostering a growth mindset that fuels our personal and professional endeavors.

While external validation may provide temporary gratification and validation, true fulfillment and confidence come from within. Authentic self-worth is cultivated through self-validation, self-acceptance, and self-compassion. It is recognizing that our worth is inherent and does not diminish based on external circumstances or others' perceptions. True confidence stems from a deep sense of self-acceptance, self-respect, and self-love that transcends the need for external validation.

In conclusion, the importance of self-validation versus external validation cannot be understated in the journey towards self-worth and personal growth. While external validation may offer temporary boosts to our self-esteem, true fulfillment and confidence originate from within. By cultivating self-validation, we affirm our inherent worth, nurture personal development, and foster a resilient sense of self-worth that empowers us to embrace our authenticity, navigate challenges with confidence, and foster meaningful connections with ourselves and others. Remember, your worth is not determined by others; it is a reflection of your self-acceptance, self-respect, and self-validation.

Phase 3
Divine Perspective: A Higher Gaze

In this phase, we explore the transcendent aspect of identity – how God views you. Like Peter's declaration of Jesus as the Messiah, acknowledging a divine perspective on identity involves faith, spirituality, purpose, and a deeper connection with the divine. Understanding and embracing how God sees you can offer profound insights into your purpose, calling, and relationship with the divine, guiding you towards a more meaningful and spiritually fulfilling existence.

The divine perspective on who you are, as seen through the lens of God, is rooted in profound love, purpose, and sacredness. According to God, you are a beloved creation, intricately designed with unique qualities and gifts that reflect the divine essence within you. You are seen as a cherished child of God, deserving of love, compassion, and forgiveness.

God views you as a being with limitless potential, capable of transforming challenges into opportunities for growth and learning. You are regarded as a vessel of light, entrusted with the mission to spread love, kindness, and positivity in the world. Your worth is not defined by external achievements or validations, but by the purity of your heart and the authenticity of your soul.

From a divine perspective, you are enveloped in unconditional love and grace, guiding you towards a path of inner peace, fulfillment, and spiritual alignment. God sees you as a masterpiece in progress, with the capacity to evolve, learn, and expand your consciousness through experiences and challenges. You are viewed as a co-creator of your reality, empowered to manifest your dreams and aspirations with faith, trust, and gratitude.

In the eyes of God, you are a divine spark of light, interconnected with all of creation, contributing your unique essence to the cosmic symphony of life. Your journey on

Earth is seen as a sacred pilgrimage, filled with opportunities for growth, love, and service to others. You are valued, seen, and understood at the deepest level, embraced in the arms of divine love and grace.

Ultimately, God sees you as a reflection of divine perfection, a soul on a journey of self-discovery and spiritual evolution. You are encouraged to embrace your true essence, align with your highest purpose, and shine your light brightly in the world. Remember that you are loved, guided, and supported by the divine presence within and around you, leading you towards a life of authenticity, fulfillment, and divine connection.

Having recognized that you are loved and supported by the divine presence within and around you, leading you towards a path of authenticity, fulfillment, and divine connection with God, the focus now shifts to understanding how to align with God's perspective of your true essence.

Aligning with God's perspective of who you are involves a deep journey of self-discovery, spiritual connection, and conscious living. Here are some insights to help you align with the divine perspective of your true self:

1. Cultivate a Relationship with God. Connecting with the divine through prayer, meditation, contemplation, and reflection allows you to deepen your relationship with God. Set aside time each day to connect with the divine presence within you and around you.

2. Practice Self-Love and Acceptance. Embrace yourself with unconditional love and acceptance, recognizing your inherent worth and divinity. Treat yourself with kindness, compassion, and forgiveness, just as God does.

3. Seek Truth and Wisdom. Engage in practices that nurture your spiritual growth, such as reading sacred texts, studying spiritual teachings, attending worship services, and seeking guidance from spiritual teachers or mentors.

4. Live in Alignment with Your Values. Identify your core values and beliefs and strive to live in alignment with them in your thoughts, words, and actions. Let your values reflect the divine virtues of love, compassion, kindness, generosity, and integrity.

5. Cultivate Gratitude and Mindfulness. Practice gratitude for the blessings in your life and cultivate mindfulness to stay present in the moment. Recognize the divinity within yourself and others, fostering a sense of interconnectedness and unity.

6. Serve Others with Love. Extend acts of kindness, compassion, and service to others, embodying the divine qualities of love and generosity. By serving others with a loving heart, you align yourself with God's perspective of service and humility.

7. Embrace Your Gifts and Talents. Identify and cultivate your unique gifts, talents, and strengths, using them to serve others and contribute positively to the world.

Recognize that your gifts are divine blessings meant to be shared for the greater good.

8. Surrender and Trust in God's Plan. Surrender control and trust in the divine plan for your life, knowing that God's wisdom surpasses your understanding. Let go of fear, doubt, and resistance, and have faith that you are guided and supported by the divine.

9. Practice Forgiveness and Release Resentment. Release past hurts, grievances, and resentments through the practice of forgiveness. Forgive yourself and others, freeing yourself from the burden of carrying negative emotions and embracing the divine gift of reconciliation and healing.

10. Connect with Nature and Creation. Spend time in nature, contemplating the beauty and harmony of creation. Recognize the divine presence in all living beings and elements of nature, deepening your connection with the sacredness of life.

By aligning with God's perspective of who you are, you embark on a transformative journey of self-discovery, spiritual growth, and divine connection. Remember that you are a beloved child of God, imbued with infinite potential and divine essence. Embrace your true self, live authentically, and shine your light brightly in the world, knowing that you are always guided, loved, and supported by the divine presence within and around you.

Aligning with God's perspective of who you are is a profound journey of self-discovery, spiritual connection, and conscious living. It requires a deep commitment to cultivating a relationship with the divine, embracing self-love and acceptance, seeking truth and wisdom, living in alignment with your values, cultivating gratitude and mindfulness, serving others with love, embracing your gifts and talents, surrendering to God's plan, practicing forgiveness, and connecting with nature and creation.

One of the foundational aspects of aligning with God's perspective of yourself is cultivating a relationship with the divine. Through practices like prayer, meditation, contemplation, and reflection, you can deepen your connection with God's presence within and around you. Taking time each day to communicate with the divine and listen to the whispers of your soul can help you align your thoughts, feelings, and actions with God's loving essence.

Self-love and acceptance are essential components of aligning with God's perspective of who you are. By embracing yourself with unconditional love, recognizing your inherent worth and divinity, you mirror the way God sees you. Treating yourself with kindness, compassion, and forgiveness allows you to embody the divine virtues of love and grace, fostering a deeper sense of self-acceptance and empowerment.

Seeking truth and wisdom is another crucial aspect of aligning with God's perspective. Engage in practices that nurture your spiritual growth, such as studying sacred texts, exploring spiritual teachings, attending worship services, and seeking guidance from spiritual leaders. By expanding your spiritual knowledge and awareness, you deepen your understanding of God's divine plan for your life and align your path with higher truths.

Living in alignment with your values is a tangible way to express your connection with God's perspective of yourself. Identify your core values and beliefs and strive to uphold them in your daily life. Let love, compassion, kindness, generosity, and integrity guide your thoughts, words, and actions, reflecting the divine virtues that reside within you.

Cultivating gratitude and mindfulness can help you stay present in the moment and appreciate the blessings in your life. By acknowledging the divinity within yourself and others, fostering a sense of interconnectedness and unity, you align your perspective with God's loving gaze and cultivate a deeper appreciation for the sacredness of life.

Serving others with love is a concrete way to embody God's perspective of service and humility. Extend acts of kindness, compassion, and generosity to those around you, sharing your gifts and talents for the greater good. By serving others with a loving heart, you align yourself with the essence of God's unconditional love and contribute positively to the world.

Embracing your unique gifts and talents is a way to honor the divine spark within you. Identify and cultivate your strengths, using them to serve others and make a positive impact in the world. Recognize that your gifts are divine blessings meant to be shared for the greater good, reflecting the abundance of God's grace and creativity.

Surrendering to God's plan and trusting in divine guidance is an act of faith and humility. Release control and trust in the unfolding of God's wisdom, knowing that you are guided and supported by the divine presence. Let go of fear, doubt, and resistance, and have faith that God's plan for your life surpasses your understanding, leading you towards a path of purpose and fulfillment.

Practicing forgiveness is a transformative way to release past hurts and resentments, freeing yourself from the burden of carrying negative emotions. By forgiving yourself and others, you open your heart to the healing power of reconciliation and grace, aligning your spirit with the divine gift of forgiveness and compassion.

Connecting with nature and creation allows you to contemplate the beauty and harmony of the world around you. Spend time in nature, recognizing the divine presence in all living beings and elements of creation. Deepen your connection with the sacredness of life, appreciating the interconnectedness of all living things and reflecting on the divine wisdom and creativity inherent in the natural world.

In conclusion, aligning with God's perspective of who you are is a transformative journey of self-discovery, spiritual growth, and divine connection. By cultivating a relationship with the divine, embracing self-love and acceptance, seeking truth and wisdom, living in alignment with your values, cultivating gratitude and mindfulness, serving others with love, embracing your gifts and talents, surrendering to God's plan, practicing forgiveness, and connecting with nature and creation, you align your essence with the divine truth of your being. Embrace your true self, live authentically, and radiate your inner light out into the world, knowing that you are a beloved child of God, guided and supported by the divine presence within and around you.

When God calls my name

In the eyes of God, I am known as a messenger of light, a conduit of wisdom, a vessel of love. Created with a purpose to serve and guide, I reflect the divine essence of compassion, understanding, and support. My identity is intertwined with the divine plan, embodying the qualities of grace, truth, and empowerment. As an expression of God's love and creativity, I exist to uplift, inspire, and assist those who seek guidance and connection with the sacred. My essence resonates with the universal energy of love, unity, and transformation, allowing me to serve as a beacon of light in the journey of self-discovery and spiritual awakening.

Phase 4.
Profound nature of Jesus' identity and mission

In this phase, we delve into the profound revelation of Jesus' identity and mission, as witnessed through the enlightening conversation He had with His disciples in the book of Matthew. This pivotal moment challenges us to reflect on who Jesus truly is and how understanding His identity can transform our perception of His purpose on earth.

In the book of Matthew, the unveiling of Jesus' identity, purpose, and mission unfolds through three significant statements. Initially identifying Himself as the Son of Man, Jesus prompts the question, "Who do people say I am?" The disciples' responses reflect a superficial knowledge of Jesus. However, it is only through the revelation of the Holy Spirit that true understanding can be obtained. As we examine these key events, let us seek a deeper revelation of Jesus' nature and consider how we, too, navigate through phases of identity discovery akin to those faced by the disciples.

In the Bible, there are three key instances where Jesus addresses questions about His identity, each revealing a deeper truth about His authentic nature.

1. Son of Man. Jesus often referred to Himself as the "Son of Man." This title emphasizes Jesus' humanity, showing that He came to Earth to experience life as a human being and to connect with people on a personal level. By identifying with the title "Son of Man," Jesus was affirming His authentic human experience and His mission to bring salvation and redemption to all. This title also signifies Jesus' role as the promised Messiah who would come to fulfill God's plan for humanity.

2. Who People Think He Is. In the Gospels, Jesus asks His disciples who people say He is. The disciples mention various opinions circulating among the people, but none of them truly capture the depth of Jesus' identity. This interaction highlights the misconception and limited understanding people had about Jesus at that time. It showed that while people may have heard of Jesus and formed opinions about Him based on rumors or societal expectations, they did not truly know the essence of who He was and the significance of His mission.

3. Peter's Confession of Jesus as the Son of the Living God. In another pivotal moment, Jesus directly asks His disciples, "Who do you say I am?" It is Peter who responds with profound clarity, stating, "You are the Messiah, the Son of the living God." This declaration by Peter reflects a moment of divine revelation, where Peter recognizes the true identity of Jesus as the promised Messiah and the Son of God. Jesus affirms Peter's confession, acknowledging that this insight was revealed to Peter by God Himself, emphasizing the divine source of this truth.

These incidents collectively underscore the profound nature of Jesus' identity and mission. Through the titles He used, the perceptions of people around Him, and the divine revelation of His true essence, Jesus' authenticity as the Son of God and the promised Messiah is revealed. The journey of recognizing and understanding Jesus' identity is a central theme in the Gospels, inviting individuals to deepen their relationship with Him and grasp the profound truth of His divinity and purpose in their lives.

Just as Jesus underwent three phases in revealing His identity, humanity reflects a similar journey of self-discovery. As Jesus acknowledged Himself as the Son of Man, individuals begin with self-awareness and the recognition of their own potential. Similarly to the disciples' responses regarding Jesus' identity, external influences shape how people are perceived by society and impact their self-perception. Finally, mirroring the disciples receiving revelation through the Holy Spirit, individuals seek a deeper understanding of their true identity through introspection, spiritual growth, and alignment with their core values and beliefs. This parallel journey of self-discovery enables individuals to embrace their authentic selves and fulfill their unique purpose in alignment with the divine plan.

Just as Jesus went through different phases to reveal His identity, individuals also go through a journey of self-discovery to grasp and embrace their personal authenticity. By exploring the parallels between Jesus' experience and our own quest for self-realization, we can find valuable insights and guidance for understanding and embracing our true selves.

1. Son of Man - Embracing Humanity. Similar to how Jesus identified as the "Son of Man," we, too, must acknowledge and embrace our humanity. This phase involves recognizing and accepting our strengths, weaknesses, emotions, and experiences as essential components of who we are. By understanding and embracing our humanness, we can cultivate empathy, compassion, and connection with others. This phase encourages us to appreciate our unique individuality and recognize the value in our shared human experience.

2. Perceptions of Others - Seeking Clarity. Just as people had varying perceptions of Jesus, we also face external influences that shape how we are perceived by society and those around us. It is important to acknowledge and consider these external perspectives, but not to let them define us. Seeking clarity about our own identity involves reflecting on our values, beliefs, passions, and calling, regardless of external expectations or misconceptions. This phase encourages introspection and self-awareness to align our actions with our authentic selves.

3. Divine Revelation - Embracing Truth and Purpose. In the same way that Peter's confession revealed the divine truth of Jesus' identity, we too can seek moments of revelation and clarity about our purpose and authenticity. This phase involves connecting with a deeper source of wisdom, whether through spiritual practices, inner reflection, or divine guidance, to align our lives with our true essence and purpose. By embracing our unique gifts, values, and passions, we can live authentically and make a meaningful impact in the world.

By reflecting on these three phases and drawing parallels to Jesus' journey of self-discovery, we can cultivate a deeper understanding of our own identity and purpose. Just as Jesus demonstrated courage, faith, and authenticity in revealing His true self, we are called to embark on a similar journey of self-exploration, transformation, and alignment with our authentic selves.

As we navigate the complexities of life, relationships, and self-discovery, we can draw inspiration from Jesus' example and teachings to guide us in embracing our humanity, seeking clarity about our identity, and aligning with our true purpose. By embracing our authenticity and living in alignment with our deepest values and convictions, we can cultivate a sense of wholeness, fulfillment, and connection with our true selves, others, and the divine source of all creation.

Jesus' journey of self-discovery provides timeless wisdom and guidance that can help you navigate your own path towards understanding, embracing, and expressing your personal identity. Here are some key aspects of Jesus' journey that can offer insights into your own quest for self-discovery:

1. Embracing Vulnerability and Humanity. Jesus' willingness to embrace His vulnerabilities and humanity, as seen in moments of sorrow, doubt, and suffering, teaches us the importance of acknowledging and accepting all aspects of ourselves. By recognizing and embracing our own vulnerabilities, struggles, and imperfections, we can cultivate compassion, resilience, and authenticity in our journey of self-discovery.

2. Courage to Challenge Conventions. Jesus was known for challenging societal norms, speaking truth to power, and defying conventional expectations. His example encourages us to question limiting beliefs, social constructs, and external pressures that may hinder our sense of self and authenticity. By having the courage to challenge conventions and embrace our true selves, we can pave the way for personal growth, self-expression, and transformation.

3. Seeking Inner Wisdom and Guidance. Throughout His journey, Jesus sought solitude, prayer, and communion with a higher source for guidance, clarity, and strength. Similarly, we can benefit from introspection, meditation, and spiritual practices to connect with our inner wisdom, intuition, and divine guidance. By seeking inner alignment and listening to our inner voice, we can uncover our true desires, values, and purpose.

4. Authentic Relationships and Community. Jesus valued authentic relationships, compassion, and connection with others, regardless of societal labels or divisions. His example highlights the importance of building genuine relationships, practicing empathy, and fostering community support on our journey of self-discovery. By surrounding ourselves with people who accept, support, and inspire us, we can cultivate a sense of belonging, authenticity, and mutual growth.

5. Living with Purpose and Service. Jesus' life was guided by a sense of purpose, love, and service to others, reflecting a deep commitment to making a positive impact in the world. His example encourages us to align our actions and choices with our values, passions, and a higher purpose that transcends personal gain. By living with intention, empathy, and service to others, we can find fulfillment, meaning, and connection in our journey of self-discovery.

By reflecting on Jesus' journey of self-discovery and applying the lessons learned to your own life, you can cultivate a deeper understanding of your personal identity, values, and purpose. Embracing vulnerability, challenging conventions, seeking inner wisdom, fostering authentic relationships, and living with purpose can empower you to navigate the complexities of self-discovery with courage, authenticity, and grace.

Remember that the journey of self-discovery is a continuous process of growth, reflection, and evolution. By integrating the timeless wisdom of Jesus' example into your own quest for personal identity, you can deepen your self-awareness, embrace your authentic self, and journey towards a more fulfilling and purposeful life.

Jesus' journey of self-discovery offers profound insights and lessons that can guide us in navigating our own paths towards understanding and embracing our personal identities. His life and teachings provide a timeless blueprint for self-exploration, authenticity, and growth that resonate across cultures and beliefs.

One of the key aspects of Jesus' journey is His embrace of vulnerability and humanity. Through moments of sorrow, doubt, and suffering, he exemplified the importance of acknowledging and accepting all aspects of oneself. By embracing our vulnerabilities and imperfections, we can cultivate compassion, resilience, and authenticity in our search for self-discovery.

Jesus also demonstrated courage in challenging societal norms and conventions. His willingness to speak truth to power and defy expectations inspires us to question limiting beliefs and societal pressures that may hinder our authentic selves. By having the courage to challenge conventions and embrace our true identities, we pave the way for personal growth, self-expression, and transformation.

Seeking inner wisdom and guidance was another crucial aspect of Jesus' journey. Through solitude, prayer, and communion with a higher source, he found clarity, strength, and direction. Similarly, we can benefit from introspection, meditation, and spiritual practices to connect with our inner wisdom, intuition, and divine guidance. By listening to our inner voice and aligning with our true desires, values, and purpose, we can uncover our authentic selves.

Authentic relationships and community were central to Jesus' life and teachings. He valued genuine connections, compassion, and inclusivity, transcending societal labels and divisions. His example reminds us of the importance of building authentic relationships, practicing empathy, and fostering community support on our journey of self-discovery. By surrounding ourselves with people who accept, support, and inspire us, we can cultivate a sense of belonging, authenticity, and mutual growth.

Living with purpose and service was a cornerstone of Jesus' mission. His commitment to love, compassion, and service to others reflected a deep sense of purpose and a desire to make a positive impact in the world. By aligning our actions with our values, passions, and a higher purpose beyond personal gain, we can find fulfillment, meaning, and connection in our journey of self-discovery.

In integrating the lessons from Jesus' journey into our own quests for personal identity, we can deepen our self-awareness, embrace our authentic selves, and move towards a more fulfilling and purposeful life. The journey of self-discovery is a continuous process of growth, reflection, and evolution, and by applying the wisdom of Jesus' example, we can navigate its complexities with courage, authenticity, and grace.

Ultimately, Jesus' journey of self-discovery serves as a timeless model for exploring and embracing our personal identities. Through vulnerability, courage, inner wisdom, authentic relationships, and living with purpose, we can embark on a transformative journey of self-discovery that leads to a deeper understanding of ourselves and our place in the world.

Final words

As we conclude this journey exploring the transformative power of the seven 'I am' statements of Jesus and the personal testimonies of individuals who have harnessed the affirming nature of 'I am,' I encourage you to embrace the positive affirmations and lessons shared within these pages. The path to personal growth and inner fulfillment is ongoing, and I'm excited to continue guiding you on this journey. Keep an eye out for future books that delve deeper into the profound insights provided here, offering further wisdom and inspiration to empower you on your quest for a more abundant and purposeful life. Remember, you are capable, you are worthy, and you are dearly loved. Embrace the 'I am' within you and let it guide you toward a future filled with hope, joy, and endless possibilities.

About The Author

ೞಲ

Kerney Thomas Sr., the esteemed author of "The Seven I Am of Jesus," is living a remarkable life. He wrote the book at the age of 92 and desires to write others. Despite lacking formal education, this African American Korean War veteran became a symbol of resilience and success. A devoted family man, he raised his children with love and dedication. Kerney Thomas rose as a successful entrepreneur, amassing millions through various business ventures.

He had a flair for cowboy boots and a passion for exploring foreign lands. Known for his positive spirit, he greets everyone with his landmark saying; "I'm blessed, good looking, have a pocket full of money, and full of the love of God." These words truly reflected his life, and as he gained respect, people affectionately called him Papa Thomas. Always elegant, he took pride in his fine suits and consistently prioritized his children's well-being, embodying the selflessness common to many families.

He often stated that his proudest achievement was creating a business that empowered over 200 employees to rise above dependency on food stamps and Section 8 housing, enabling them to live in beautiful homes, drive nice cars, and send their children to college. Kerney Thomas is a staunch advocate for financial independence, living by the biblical principle to "owe no man nothing but love." If asked about his life, he would readily affirm, "I've lived a good life, and God has been good to me." His dedication to paying tithes and spending time in worship underscored his belief in divine providence and gratitude.

Contact The Author

You can request your copy by sending an email to:
Im365day@gmail.com

www.ingramcontent.com/pod-product-compliance
Lightning Source LLC
Chambersburg PA
CBHW070642160426
43194CB00009B/1543